Journal of Research
of the
American Federation
of Astrologers

2017

Copyright 2017 by American Federation of Astrologers
All rights reserved.

No part of this book may be reproduced or transcribed in any form or by any means, electronic or mechanical, including photocopying or recording or by any information storage and retrieval system without written permission from the author and publisher, except in the case of brief quotations embodied in critical reviews and articles. Requests and inquiries may be mailed to: American Federation of Astrologers, Inc., 6535 S. Rural Road, Tempe, AZ 85283.

ISBN-10: 0-86690-663-0
ISBN-13: 978-0-86690-663-0

Cover Design: Jack Cipolla

Published by:
American Federation of Astrologers, Inc.
6535 S. Rural Road
Tempe, AZ 85283

www.astrologers.com

Contents

From the Editor	v
On Lawyers' Astrological Factors By Kyösti Tarvainen, Ph.D	1
Jung on Astrology: Gathering Constellations By Safron Rossi, PhD	11
Earthquake Prediction: Model IV By Jagdish Maheshri	37
Sun Square Neptune: Narcissism vs. Quietism: Can We Change the Narrative? By Branimira Maldeghem	73
Predicting Weather with Astrology By Alphee Lavoie	107
Nergal: The Shaping of the God Mars in Sumer, Assyria, and Babylon By José Luis Belmonte	125
Esoteric Jewish Astrology By Karni Zor	
Astrology of the Sequester: Obama's 20-hour Standoff and the Difference It Made By Sylvia Sky	145
Qualitative Research: Narrative Report on the Personal Lunar Cycle By Aureal Williams	153
Domestic Terrorism: 2016 Was a Difficult Year By Marilyn J. Muir, LPMAFA	173
About the Authors	199

From the Editor

The American Federation of Astrologers is proud to publish the papers from the second year recipients of the Catharine and Ernest Grant Trust Astrological Research Grants. The monetary awards from the Grant Trust were made to Jagdish Mahashri, Safron Rossi, and Branimira Maldeghem for the purpose of furthering astrological research. They are members of the American Federation of Astrologers (AFA), the International Society of Astrological Research (ISAR), and the National Council for Geocosmic Research (NCGR).

As part of the AFA's educational mission, the AFA will present a workshop entitled "Research Approaches for Astrology Projects" at the United Astrology Conference in May 2018 to be held in Chicago. This is designed as an introductory presentation to the various kinds of research questions and the appropriate methods and resources that can help the novice research astrologer develop a plan to investigate his or her inquiry.

In addition to these grant recipient studies, this research journal includes several noteworthy papers from the general membership of the AFA. They represent investigations of astrologers from around the world, with submissions from Finland, Israel, Bulgaria, Spain, India, and the United States. The broad categories of research that these papers address employ quantitative and qualitative methods as well as hybrid and historical approaches that expand the body of astrological knowledge and understanding.

We are honored to open this journal with a study by the mathematician, statistician, and systems analyst Kyosti Tarvainen, Ph.D. from Finland who investigates the factors that may be prominent in the charts of Finnish lawyers. He speculates that the instances where the results vary from the expected norm might be attributed differences in the court system and admission procedures to the law schools in the USA and Finland.

Safron Rossi, Ph.D. is an associate core faculty member at Pacific Graduate Institute and is NCGR's choice for the Grant Award. Acknowledging the influence of C.G. Jung's psychology upon many psychological and archetypal approaches to contemporary astrology, she presents a selection of passages from his works about his thoughts on an astrological worldview. Her forthcoming book, *Jung and Astrology* (Routledge) will be available in 2017.

Jagdish Maheshri, Ph.D., the director of research for the NCGR and the AFA recipient for the Grant Award. He is a chemical engineer and contemporary Vedic astrologer living in both India and the U.S. His paper is a continuation of his ongoing research investigating the correlations between astronomical data and earthquakes. In this study he explores if any correlation exists between the declination angles of planets and the occurrence of strong earthquakes of magnitude 7 and higher.

Branimira Maldeghem is ISAR's representative for the Grant Award. She has a M.A. in political science and public administration and has worked as a consultant for various NGOs and political parties in Bulgaria. Her paper explores the psychological dynamics of Sun square Neptune as reflected in the life experiences and artistic works of the French filmmaker Jean-Luc Godard, testing the theoretical paradigm of AstroPsychology, as developed by Glenn Perry, PhD.

Alphee Lavoie, developer of AIR Software and founder of the Astro Investigators, shares his research in the field of natural astrology on predicting weather for a certain locality. He tests the accuracy of the method of weather prediction described in the Church of Light book *Weather Predicting* by C.C. Zain by investigating the planetary influences operative in each quarter moon for each month of the year.

Jose Luis Belmonte lives in Barcelona, Spain, and earned a M.A. from Kepler College, and researches the history of Babylonian and Hellenistic astrology. His paper examines the latest findings about the Babylonian god *Nergal* in the field of Assyriology and history of the Near East. He poses that this Babylonian deity is the basis for the derivation the astrological meaning of the Greco-Roman god Mars (Ares in Greek).

Karni Zor from Israel has a B.A in archaeology and M.A. in theological studies. Her paper on esoteric Jewish astrology explores the ways that astrology was practiced and embedded in the Jewish tradition and historical religious texts, even though it has been forbidden in some orthodox sects.

Sylvia Sky is a prolific writer for many astrological publications. She presents a study of the Congressional order known as the "sequester," mandating automatic U.S. federal budget cuts. Her inquiry focuses upon an analysis of the chart at the time when Congress said the order would go into effect and the actual time when President Obama signed the order and how that changed the course and final outcome of this legislation.

Aureal Williams, whose background is in the field of holistic health nursing, shares a 21-year narrative working with the personal lunar cycle, based upon the Sun-Moon angle at birth. She describes how scheduling life in accordance with this cycle increases synchronicity and decreases stress related to a strengthened sense of connection with the cosmos.

Marilyn J. Muir, professional astrologer, instructor, writer, and media commentator, turns to the field of mundane astrology with her exploration of three acts of domestic terrorism that all occurred on the same day, September 17, 2016. She focused her study upon the identification of common degrees in these charts that joined major long-range stress aspects such as Uranus square Pluto in cardinal signs and Saturn square Neptune in mutable signs.

The American Federation of Astrologers extends its appreciation to these contributors for their hard work and dedication in furthering the body of astrological knowledge.

Demetra George
Research Director
American Federation of Astrologers

On Lawyers' Astrological Factors

By Kyösti Tarvainen, Ph.D

ABSTRACT: Astrological factors of lawyers are studied from two perspectives. First, Robert Pelletier mentions (*Planets in Aspect*, 1974), in connection of 44 aspects, that the aspect is suitable for the lawyer's profession. Among 17,765 Finnish lawyers, these aspects were not more common than expected in a statistically significant way. As a reason for this result, one can see the differences in the court system and admission procedures to the law schools in the United States and Finland. When correspondingly a part of Pelletier's aspects, chiefly martial ones, were left out, the remaining 31 aspects were common among the Finnish lawyers in a statistically significant way ($p = 0.04$). Second, the lawyer's profession is very mercurial like that of journalists. Sakoian and Acker (*The Astrologer's Handbook*, 1973) mention favorable astrological factors for journalists. These are mental factors related to Mercury and Gemini. It turned out that, among the Finnish lawyers, these mental factors were more common than expected in a statistically significant way ($p = 0.04$). One may expect that an excess of mental astrological factors is a common feature of lawyers in all countries.

Introduction

Aspects are a good subject for astrological statistical studies since they are strong factors and many of them last so many days that it is enough to know the birth date (whereby one uses the noon time for calculating the chart).

For example, an aspect study by Tarvainen (2015) considered 6,285 Finnish theologians. They had a statistically significant excess of 11 Jupiter aspects regarded as propitious for theologians by Pelletier (1974). Another aspect study (including also some sign factors) considered 2,759 famous mathematicians born after 1700 (Tarvainen, 2013). They had a statistically significant excess of 17 factors that according to Sakoian and Acker (1973) support mathematicians.

In the present study, it is first checked whether the 44 aspects said favorable by Pelletier (1974) for lawyers are more common than expected among the 17,765 Finnish lawyers who have a master's degree in law (Finnish lawyers, 2011). The aspects mentioned by Pelletier are indicated in Table 1. Second, the mentality of the lawyers is considered.

Research Method

To determine the excess of the Pelletier's 44 aspects among the Finnish lawyers, control groups representing the whole population were generated with the *shuffling* method. This is a widely applicable method for generating control groups in astrological research (cf., for example, Ruis, 2007/2008; Tarvainen, 2012).

In the basic form of shuffling, a control group of the same size as the data is generated by taking the dates (date and month together), years, birth times, and places independently in random order without replacement. In this basic scheme, the positions of the Sun are replicated in the control groups. Therefore, sometimes somewhat more accurate results can be obtained by adding such random changes to the obtained birthdays that do not essentially change the yearly distribution of birthdays. In the present study, random changes varying from -90 to +90 days were added to the birth dates.

The shuffling was repeated 1,000 times, whereby the average values related to these shuffled groups did not change significantly when more shuffled groups were generated.

The excess of the 44 aspects in the data is obtained as the difference between the total amount of the 44 aspects in the data and the corresponding average in the 1,000 control groups of the size of the data. When we talk about control values for a data set, we mean the average values for the 1,000 control groups.

Then the p-value for the obtained excess—indicating the probability that this excess has arisen by pure chance—can be estimated in the following ways (cf., for example, Ruis, 1993/1994; Tarvainen, 2012).

The p-value can often be estimated for the 44 aspects directly by determining the total number of the 44 aspects in each of the 1,000 control groups of the size of the data and by observing how many of these total numbers is at least as big as that in the data.

But if the p-value is so small that it can't be estimated in this direct way, a Normal distribution approximation can usually be made for the distribution of these 1,000 total numbers. Thereby, the mean value and the standard deviation of the 1,000 total numbers are determined and used as parameters in a Normal distribution approximation. The p-value is then obtained, using this Normal distribution, as the probability that the total number in the control group has a higher or the same value as in the data.

Results for Pelletier's Aspects

The orbs suggested by the Faculty of Astrological Studies (Tompkins, 1989, p. 66) were used for the aspects. For conjunctions, oppositions, trines, and squares, the orb is 8°; for sextiles, 4°; and an additional 2° for aspects involving the Sun or Moon. The mentioned 44 aspects did have a tiny excess 0.1% among the 17,765 lawyers, but this excess was not statistically significant (p = 0.38). Table 1 presents the excesses and p-values for different planet pairs.

Table 1. Excess of aspects mentioned suitable for lawyers by Pelletier (1974).

The data contains 17 765 Finnish lawyers. For example, the first number 2.4% means that the total number of the Sun-Mars aspects indicated in the first column is 2.4% higher in the data than in the control groups. The number 0.02 (= 2%) in the third column describes the probability that this excess has occurred by chance. For example, the notion SO-90-MA means that the angle between the Sun and Mars is 90° (the orbs are given in the text).

Aspect	Excess (+) or deficit (-) of aspects	p-value
SO-0-MA, SO-90-MA, SO-120-MA, SO-180-MA	+ 2.4%	0.02
SO-0-JU, SO-60-JU, SO-90-JU, SO-120-JU	0.0001	0.49
SO-0-SA, SO-60-SA, SO-120-SA, SO-180-SA	+ 0.9%	0.21
ME-0-MA, ME-60-MA, ME-90-MA, ME-120-MA, ME-180-MA	−1.1%	0.84
ME-120-JU, ME-180-JU	+ 2.4%	0.12
VE-0-SA, VE-60-SA, VE-90-SA, VE-120-SA, VE-180-SA	− 0.7%	0.74
MA-0-JU, MA-60-JU, MA-90-JU, MA-120-JU, MA-180-JU	− 1.2%	0.86

JU-0-SA, JU-60-SA, JU-90-SA, JU-120-SA, JU-180-SA	0.002	0.41
JU-0-UR, JU-60-UR, JU-90-UR, JU-120-UR, JU-180-UR	+0.8%	0.22
JU-0-PL, JU-60-PL	+2.5%	0.10
VE-60-PL	-3.0%	0.80
MA-120-NE	-2.0%	0.80
SA-120-NE	-0.4%	0.61
All above 44 aspects together	+0.1%	0.38
31 aspects (leaving out MA-JU and MA-ME aspects and VE-60-PL, MA-120-NE, SA-120-NE)	+0.8%	0.04

One possible reason for not obtaining statistical significance is the difference between the United States and Finnish court systems. Pelletier's aspect list has a strong Mars emphasis, possibly because in the United States courts personal appearance with confident opinions (MA-JU) and repartee (MA-ME) are important. In Finland, there are no such juries as in the United States, but lay members who, in serious crime cases, discuss the verdict with the professional judge or judges. The handling of matters in the court is based much on written material. The Finnish lawyers are clearly not as martial as the United States lawyers.

Also, admission procedures to law schools are different in the United States and Finland. In both countries, the admission is based on earlier school grades and some tests. But in Finland, the admission tests are much harder, since, before them, one has to read 500-1,000 pages of dry law text, on which the test questions are prepared. Most applicants take a commercial preparatory course. Fewer than 20 percent of the applicants are accepted. This hard Finnish admission system probably ensures that Finnish lawyers are more saturnine and less martial on average than their United States colleagues.

Now, thinking of these cultural differences, we modify Pelletier's aspect list. We leave out the mentioned martial MA-JU and MA-ME aspects for Finnish lawyers. The MA-SO aspects still remain, relating to general energy and independent character of lawyers.

Furthermore, we leave out the following single aspects, which perhaps also could be ignored in the United States: VE-60-PL since this is mentioned only in connection of lawyers in the field of wills and trusts; MA-120-NE and SA-120-NE since Pelletier suggest the legal profession for persons having these Neptune aspects very much for idealistic reasons.

It turned out that the remaining 31 aspects have a statistically significant ($p = 0.04$) excess of 0.8% among the Finnish lawyers.

It is interesting to note that when Pelletier mentions, for a planet pair, at least two aspects, then there is about the same excess for all five Ptolemaic aspects (0°, 60°, 90°, 120°, 180°). When we consider, instead of the 31 aspects, all the 40 Ptolemaic aspects of the planet pairs SO-MA, SO-JU, SO-SA, ME-JU, VE-SA, JU-SA, JU-UR, and JU-PL, the excess is 0.6% with a p-value 0.04. This is a confirmation to the starting point of *Aspects in Astrology* (1989) by Tompkins, where the central thing in an aspect is its planets, not the angle between them.

Consequently, in further lawyer studies in other countries, one could consider these 40 Ptolemaic aspects, plus possibly the ten MA-ME and MA-JU Ptolemaic aspects which seemed to be too martial for Finnish lawyers.

Mentality of Lawyers

In addition to Pelletier's aspects, we pay attention to the fact that the lawyer's profession is very mental. In fact, *The Rulership Book* (1971) by Rex Bills mentions Mercury as a lawyers' ruling planet in addition to Jupiter, which is commonly connected to justice.

To obtain an authoritative list of mental astrological factors, we can notice that the legal and journalism professions have a similar mental nature. Both vocations include much reading and interviewing, going into the matters in greater detail, making conclusions, and writing summaries and presenting them. Sakoian and Acker mention, in connection with 26 astrological factors, that the factor is propitious for journalists. They are all mental factors related to Mercury, Gemini, and the third house. Due to the similarity of the professions of the journalists and lawyers, we may expect that these mercurial factors are propitious and common also in the case of lawyers.

Some of these factors require the knowledge of the birth hour. But without significant inaccuracies we can use the noon times and consider the following 15 factors: Sun, Mercury, Mars, Jupiter or Saturn in Gemini, Mercury in Virgo, ME-0-MA, ME-120-MA, ME-0-VE, ME-60-VE, MO-60-ME, ME-60-SA, ME-120-SA, ME-120-JU, and ME-120-PL.

It turned out that there was a 1% excess of these 15 mental factors among the Finnish lawyers and it was statistically significant ($p = 0.04$).

I addition to the above 15 mental factors, there was also a strong excess in the following factors enhancing mental faculties:

- Moon in Gemini: excess 7%, $p = 0.004$
- Mars in Gemini: excess 8%, $p = 0.0005$
- Mercury in Aries: excess 8%, $p = 0.0004$
- Sun in Virgo: excess 5%, $p = 0.02$
- Excess of the air element 0.7%, $p = 0.03$

In further studies of lawyers, one could enlarge the list of the 15 mental factors due to Sakoian and Acker with these five factors, whereby one would have 20 factors.

It should be noted that Sakoian and Acker did not present a

list for journalists (nor did Pelletier for lawyers). Sakoian and Acker just mention journalists as an example when treating some astrological factors. For the Moon in Gemini, they did not mention any vocation, evidently because Moon in Gemini is propitious for so many professions. But if they had written a list of good factors for journalists, they might have mentioned the Moon in Gemini and many other factors.

There was an excess also in the following mental factors, but not as strong as in the above five factors: Sun in Gemini, Mercury in Ptolemaic aspects to Saturn, Uranus, Neptune, and Pluto.

Besides mental factors, it was striking that in this data there was an excess of Uranus' Ptolemaic aspects to all other planets than Pluto. This could be checked in further studies.

Another surprising observation was that the Finnish lawyers had an excess of Ptolemaic VE-NE aspects, even if not in a statistically significant way ($p = 0.19$). The lawyers are often considered as hard-hearted persons. But the excess of the idealistic VE-NE aspects may tell that, for some of the lawyers, the goal of promoting justice has been a motivation to the vocation: in addition to Jupiter, Venus (and its ruling sign Libra) is regarded as a ruler of justice (Bills, 1971). The present Finnish president is a lawyer with a Venus-Neptune square.

Discussion

It is more difficult to study astrologically lawyers than theologians and mathematicians. First, the persons in last mentioned two groups have special characters and capabilities, whereas virtually every rational person can become a lawyer.

Second, lawyers work in diverse workplaces partly reflecting their different characters: in courts as judges, prosecutors, and attorneys for the defense; in law schools; in politics and government; in private lawyer's offices; in companies and various organizations.

Third, there are differences in the legal systems and admission procedures to law schools in different countries. Evidently for these two reasons, Pelletier's original list of 44 good aspects did not have statistical significance for Finnish lawyers, but by playing down especially the strong Mars in the list, it worked in Finland. It would be interesting to see if the original list is statistically significant in the United States and other countries.

The lawyer's profession is very mental. And it was noted that among the Finnish lawyers mental astrological factors are strong in a statistically significant way. Lawyers' mental factors can be expected to be strong in every country.

In astrology, the birth time is very important. Nowadays the big Gauquelin data sets containing birth times are available on the net. With the help of them, statistically significant results have been obtained in over ten studies (cf., Snow, 2016). But the present study plus the studies concerning theologians and mathematicians are an encouragement that interesting results can be obtained also in aspect studies (which may include sign factors) even if the birth times are not known.

Bibliography

Bills, Rex E., *The Rulership Book* (Virginia: Macoy Publishing, 1971).
Finnish lawyers, *Suomen lakimiehet* (Helsinki: Talentum, 2011).
Pelletier, R., *Planets in Aspect* (Massachusetts: Para Research, 1974).
Ruis, J., "Indication for a role of synastry aspects in a Gauquelin-sample of 2824 marriages (I)," *Correlation,* 12(2), 20–43 (1993/1994).
Ruis, J., "Statistical analysis of the birth charts of serial killers," *Correlation,* 25(2), 7–44 (2007/2008).
Sakoian, F., and L. S. Acker, *The Astrologer's Handbook* (New York: Harper Perennial, 1973).
Snow, Edward, "New Tests with Gauquelin Data Confirm Astrology," *Astrology News Service*, October 18, 2016, http://astrologynewsservice.com/articles/new-tests-with-gauquelin-data-con-

firm-astrology/, accessed November 2016.

Tarvainen, K., "Henning's synthesis method shows validity of astrology in the Gauquelins' data," *Correlation,* 28(1), 25–43 (2012).

Tarvainen, K., "Favorable astrological factors for mathematicians," *Correlation* 29(1): 39-51 (2013).

Tarvainen, K., "A study of major and minor aspects in theologians' charts," *Correlation* 30(1): 29-36 (2015).

Tompkins, S., *Aspects in Astrology* (Dorset: Element Books, 1989).

***

Data is available at kyosti.tarvainen@gmail.com.

Jung on Astrology[1]: Gathering Constellations

By Safron Rossi, PhD

ABSTRACT: C.G. Jung's psychology has been a significant influence in branches of psychological astrology. Yet within that field and beyond little is known of what Jung actually wrote on the subject itself. The research undertaken for the NCGR Grant Trust grant was dedicated to compiling extracts from Jung's writings pertaining to astrology into a book. This book brings together in a single volume Jung's writings on this topic, organized into themes, and his reflections on the relationship of the psyche to the cosmos, which is central to understanding an astrological worldview. In this research paper I share some ideas about Jung and astrology from the introduction of the forthcoming book, and then present a selection of passages of Jung's from each of the astrological symbolism chapters that are particularly rich in regards to his thoughts on astrology. The following is from the forthcoming *Jung on Astrology*, Eds. Safron Rossi and Keiron Le Grice. London, UK: Routledge, 2017.

The astrological horoscope, Carl Jung wrote in a letter of 1954, "corresponds to a definite moment in the colloquy of the gods, that is to say psychic archetypes." This statement, one of many similar assertions made throughout his life, is illustrative of Jung's belief that astrology can provide symbolic insight into the workings of the human psyche. Astrological charts, cast for specific moments in time, might be construed as something like a portrayal of the principles, or archetypes, once represented by gods and goddesses of ancient myth. Indeed, astrology, he remarked to Sigmund Freud, "seems indispensable for a proper understanding of mythology." However, despite Jung's fascination with and sustained exploration of astrology, his views on the subject have received scant attention from scholars in the field, especially compared to other comparable topics, such as alchemy and synchronicity. By contrast, Jung's ideas have been readily embraced by many practicing astrologers and authors of astrology books, perhaps in the hope that Jung might lend to astrology a degree of credibility otherwise lacking. This book—a compilation of Jung's writings in this area—is intended for readers in both fields: depth psychology and astrology. Yet the ideas explored herein are also relevant to any of us searching for deeper life meaning and a greater sense of order in life, or for a way to explore the mysteries of human experience.

Questions of the human being's place within the cosmos, of the limits of rationality and causal determinism, and of the scope of human free will and the existence of what was once called fate or destiny, remain critically relevant to us today, especially in light of the unprecedented global crises confronting us. Now, as in other periods of our recent past, the challenges of our historical moment impress upon us the need to better recognize and work in harmony with the greater forces, both psychological and physical, shaping our lives. "We know nothing of man," Jung proclaimed in an interview near the end of this life, and it is this unconsciousness of the deeper dimensions of human nature that, he believed, poses the greatest threat to our existence, and perhaps today even to the planet's. No less significant is the need to find sources of individual life meaning and orientation for our future direction, given the increasing secularism of the modern world and the much-discussed absence of myth and decline of religion. In giving his attention to the symbolism, practice, and theoretical understanding of astrology, throughout the course of his long life C. G. Jung grappled with each of these concerns. The results of his exploration of astrology, recorded in various places in Jung's *Collected Works* and his other less formal writing, is set before you in this volume.

Such is the intricate connection between astrology and Jungian ideas that the compilation of Jung's writings on this topic also constitutes an excursion into many, if not all, of the central aspects of his psychology, encompassing his theories of archetypes and the collective unconscious, individuation, synchronicity, symbolism and myth, alchemy, the evolution of the God-image, and more. Perhaps this range is not so surprising when we take into account Jung's view that astrology represents "the sum of all the psychological knowledge of antiquity."[2] For it could be argued that in certain respects Jungian psychology represents a modern articulation of the concerns of symbolic systems and practices omitted from the modern scientific worldview, astrology and alchemy chief among them. At root, both astrology and Jungian psychology might be seen as engaged with the critical task of developing greater self-knowledge, of bringing to awareness the unconscious factors underlying our life experience. In Jung's view, astrology—whatever else it might be—is a symbolic language of archetypes, the formative principles and patterns in the depths of the unconscious mind.

While numerous astrological books have drawn on perspectives and ideas in Jungian psychology, as noted far less is known about Jung's own thoughts on astrology, which are often buried within discussions of other ideas and scattered across the many volumes of his *Collected Works* and other publications. This book is intended to address the need for an exposition of his ideas within a single volume, allowing Jung to speak for himself, as it were, and thus perhaps to extricate Jung's own reflections on astrology from the ways Jungian ideas have been used by astrological writers. It is hoped that the book will allow readers to see for themselves Jung's enduring fascination with the topic, and to read firsthand his own reflections on it, so as to be able to evaluate astrology's significance within the larger corpus of his work and assess its potential relevance for our time.

Astrology for Jung was another of the controversial topics—along with the paranormal, synchronicity, alchemy, and UFO symbolism—that occupied his attention for much of this life, evident as early as 1911 in correspondence with Freud ("my evenings are taken up very largely with astrology")[3] to his many letters on this topic from the late 1950s. The concentration of letters on synchronicity, astrology, the paranormal, etc. between 1954 and 1959, occurred during a Uranus-square-Neptune world transit. Initially, this was aligned with Jung's Jupiter (1954) and then with his Neptune and Sun (1958). Jung's writing in this area is of historical and biographical import too, revealing Jung's engagement with astrology as one notable element of a burgeoning cultural interest in the irrational and the psychological in the late nineteenth and early twentieth centuries, a movement out of which depth psychology itself arose. At a biographical level, Jung's fascination with astrology, and other aspects of the occult, was a contributory factor in his professional and personal break from Sigmund Freud in early 1913. Jung's interest in matters astrological was to continue in the decades to follow, especially evident in seminars given in the late 1920s and 1930s, and then in letters and formal writing from the 1950s, in connection with synchronicity, modern physics, and reflections on the mind-matter relationship. Although not treated in a dedicated volume of the *Collected Works*, astrology occupied

Jung's attention for a fifty-year period as he grappled with its workings and applied its symbolism to illuminate both individual psychology and the evolution of mythic symbolism across Western civilization.

The Significance of Jungian Psychology in Astrology

The influence of Jungian thought in psychological astrology has been pivotal. It has provided a theoretical orientation that includes the reality of the unconscious and the importance of symbolic ways of knowing thereby giving access to the archetypal imagination and its divine data. Jungian psychology has recovered the value of mythological ideas and revived a sense of the cosmological as a factor in psychic welling being. When the celestial realm is held as a meaningful mirror to the soul there one experiences an sense of alignment with the deeper levels of life, as well as a sense of being a small part of a greater consciousness.

Prominent astrologers who cite Jung as an authority and have used Jungian ideas in their work include Liz Greene, Stephen Arroyo, Karen Hamaker-Zondag, Alice O. Howell and Richard Tarnas. Whereas these astrologers have their unique approaches to articulating Jung's thought in relation to astrology, we find there are three main ways in which Jungian psychology has been employed: guide to psychological interpretation of astrological factors, to emphasize psychological development (rather than offer prediction, as in traditional astrology), and for setting forth the theoretical assumptions behind astrology.

That Jung's analytical psychology has become a touchstone for the interpretation of astrological factors is evidenced in the many books that attempt to synthesize the two fields. One place where the two fields meet is in the manner astrological elements and zodiac signs correspond to Jung's four psychological types. Whereas Jung opened the door between typology and other ancient theories of character classification, he didn't pursue the correlation to astrology. While Stephen Arroyo was one of the early astrologers to link Jung's psychology of archetypes and astrology and the four elements, Jung's theory of typology was first correlated to the astrological elements by Jungian analyst and astrologer Liz Greene in *Relating*. She writes "Jung's four function types fit hand in glove with astrology's ancient division of the four elements. It is not a case of one being explained away by, or derived from, the other; rather, each is a distinct way of describing the empiric observations of the same phenomena".[4] Greene relates the element of air to the thinking type, water to the feeling type, earth to the sensation type, and fire to the intuitive type. These type to element correlations of Greene's have become canonical in psychological astrology. Karen Hamaker-Zondag, also a Jungian analyst and astrologer, has likewise written in depth on the correspondence between Jung's typology and the elements.

Jung's concept of the shadow and its relation to the planet Saturn is another example of psycho-astrological synthesis. Personifying the negative side of the personality, the shadow is composed of those aspects which one represses and hides from oneself, often experienced in projection. Jung said that owning one's shadow and reconciling to it in some manner, is the first step of psychological work, for within the darkest aspects of our nature lies the potential for integration and wholeness. The shadow has been correlated to the planet Saturn since this planet is related to the processes of contraction, limitation, as well as discipline, fear, and the *prima materia* of the alchemical work. At the same time Saturn is the wise old one, the master, the great teacher. Both of these faces can be seen in the concept of the shadow. The correspondences are most notably explored in Liz Greene's two books *Saturn: A New Look at An Old Devil* and *Relating*. She writes, "The position of Saturn on the birth chart suggests a sphere of the individual's life in which he has been somehow stunted, or arrested in growth, in which he may well feel inadequate, oversensitive or clumsy . . . [as]the unconscious side of personality is built up partially of those qualities which belong to us but which we cannot, or dare not, express. We may thus infer from the placement of Saturn that area where the shadow will express itself most readily, where one is perhaps the most defensive and critical of others, and where one is most liable to attract the hostility and opposition of the environment because of one's own unconscious attitude of inferiority".[5] Alice O. Howell, Jungian analyst and astrologer, has also written about the relationship between the darker and repressed aspects of the psyche and Saturn's archetypal influence. "When Saturn pairs up with any other planetary process and furthers its negative expression you will find one of the 'seven deadly sins' or, psychologically expressed, one of the repressed or suppressed complexes. . . . Complexes are not in themselves sins but the results of processes which have been in intense internal conflict, for one reason or another, causing the go to suffer a lack of harmony and self-acceptance".[6] While these darker faces of Saturn signify his importance in a chart, his role in individuation is paramount. It is through Saturn that we learn what the soul most deeply needs, and he is also the teacher whose lessons bring opportunities for profound growth and maturity.[7] Saturn is both what is working us, and that part of our psyche that must be worked. As Jung often noted, the shadow is the doorway into the unconscious. In metaphorical terms, it is lead (Saturn) that is transformed into gold by those arduous and wondrous alchemical processes.

Astrology as a guide to psychological development is expressed in a number of ways, foremost being the perspective that the birth chart is symbolic of an individual's soul, revealing how a person experiences life, the nature of their complexes, and their calling. Alice Howell writes that the birth chart "is, *in potentia*, a treasure map to the individuation process or greater awareness of the Self, and I am using Self in Jung's definition of the word as meaning the center and totality of the psyche. The chart will impel us unconsciously, as do out complexes, until we become more conscious".[8] Thus working with one's chart as a symbol becomes a tool for psychological growth for one can explore with some objectivity one's character, wounds, challenges and calling. Furthermore, from this perspective the regular transits that one experiences, particularly of the outer planets (and progressions) are understood to function as thresholds of transformations of consciousness. Correlating to natural stages of aging and maturity, the planetary archetypes reflect psychological stages and opportunities for growth. This is related to Jung's concept of individuation, which is a spiritual journey wherein unconscious and conscious elements of the psyche become integrated.

Lastly, some of Jung's ideas have become critical contributions to working with the theoretical assumptions behind astrology. The influence of Jung's ontological understanding of the archetypal basis of reality and the role of synchronicity in the emerging astrological worldview is best articulated currently in archetypal cosmology and astrology, a field pioneered by Richard Tarnas. In *Cosmos and Psyche*, Tarnas lays out these two foundational ideas of Jung and presents a worldview that is based upon the archetypal principles that synchronistically underlie and inform all of life, which he argues is evidenced in the astrological paradigm. "Between the astronomical and human is an archetypally informed synchronicity"[9] Tarnas writes. This is one of the most important contributions of Jung's thought to contemporary development and research in astrology, one which is introduced in greater detail in part IV of this volume.

Arroyo's thoughts on what astrology offers summarizes the main sensibilities of a Jungian psychological approach to astrology. Contemporary western people have "lost touch with the archetypal foundation of [their] being and with the source of support and spiritual-psychological nourishment which they provide. Astrology can be used as a way of reuniting man [sic] with his innermost self, with nature, and with the evolutionary process of the universe".[10]

Organization of the Book

Among the possible ways the material might have been presented to the reader, we chose to organize by theme rather than chronologically or reproducing Jung's writings on astrology as they appear volume by volume. In many of his reflections, scattered throughout the *Collected Works* and elsewhere, Jung proffers an eclectic assortment of thoughts on the topic, intermingled with reflections on other subjects. On occasion, he even shifts position on his views of astrology within the space of a single chapter or section. While such fluctuations are of themselves noteworthy, they are not conducive to clear understanding and there is little in the way of a discernible evolution of his ideas on astrology leading to a consistent position, which might have justified presenting the ideas in strict chronological sequence. Thus, rather than presenting Jung's words in the entire context in which they appear in the source texts, we took the decision to extract particular sentences or paragraphs, where appropriate, in order to present material in discrete parts and chapters, although material in one section unavoidably overlaps with that in other sections. The reader can refer to the original sources if a fuller appreciation of context is needed. In organizing the material by theme, we hoped to achieve a logical continuity of ideas and as much coherence as possible.

Although certain passages have been omitted to minimize repetition, almost all of Jung's writing on astrology is incorporated into this volume, sourced from the *Collected Works*, his transcribed seminars (*Visions, Nietzsche's Zarathustra*, and *Dream Analysis*), the two volumes of his letters, and the *Red Book*. One omission is the statistical data and analysis comprising Jung's ill-conceived astrological experiment, which is presented in full in the monograph "Synchronicity: An Acausal Connecting Principle." Rather than repeat the data here, which is notable primarily for its methodological flaws and statistical errors, we chose instead to include only relevant interpretive and theoretical material from the monograph, such as Jung's oscillation as to whether or not to view astrology as a mantic method.

More material from the volumes on alchemy might have been included in this book too, but in our estimation astrological symbolism in alchemy can be more appropriately approached through a study of the latter; in most cases, Jung's astrological references in his alchemical writings can only be adequately appreciated in the context of the often complicated exegeses and interpretations in *Psychology and Alchemy*, *Alchemical Studies*, and *Mysterium Coniunctionis*. Nonetheless, we have included here select material from these books, such as Jung's reflections on *Heimarmene* as astrological fate and archetypal compulsion.

Part II: Astrological Symbolism in Jung's Writings

The three chapters that comprise this section illustrate how astrology was one of the rich symbolic systems from which Jung would draw in his amplifications of psychological material, whether personal or collective. "Amplificatory interpretation," writes Murray Stein, "as a therapeutic technique serves to save, or to restore, meaning and to ground individual experience in archetypal patterns."[11] Connecting the personal and archetypal are essential in meaning-making and in personal myth because then the individual is connected to the river of life that extends beyond the personal into what is both deeply human and transpersonal at the same time.

The chapter on planetary and zodiacal symbolism is a collection of many passages from throughout Jung's writings that displays the analogical richness of astrological symbolism in his thought, illustrating his amplificatory process, which was in service to opening up or deepening the topic at hand.

Since astrology was not a subject that Jung took up in the same in-depth way he did with alchemy, the reader will encounter pockets of insight organized around certain symbols rather than a comprehensive and equal exploration of zodiacal symbols or the planets. It may be noted that Jung almost exclusively focused on the traditional planets known to antiquity, therefore there is no material related to what is called the "transpersonal" or collective planets Uranus, Neptune and Pluto. This chapter may be best engaged by dipping in and out, like a bird hovering over the surface of the sea waiting for her catch. Jung's insights are distinct and episodic, not systematized.

The astrological parallels to psychology come in succinct phrases. Jung wrote, "The psychic life-force, the libido, symbolizes itself in the sun or personifies itself in figures of heroes with solar attributes."[12] Here he connects the psychological concept of libido or psychic energy to the symbol of the astrological sun and its solar hero personifications. In the mythological nature of the psyche, the goddesses and gods, heroes, dramatic plots and themes are metaphors of the psyche's activity. Myths are metaphoric descriptions of the psyche's processes, and reveal the unconscious. So we turn to myth, literature and art in order to access and better understand the psyche and our inner processes. The relevance of mytho-astrological research in psychological astrology is based on this primary principle of Jung's psychology. Here are some excerpts of Jung's from this chapter.

Signs of the Zodiac

From: Lecture VIII, "27 November 1929," in *Dream Analysis*, 404

This is the way the signs go:

Aquarius: Five thousand years ago, 3000 B.C. when the sun was in winter, there were floods of rain. Aquarius walked about pouring his water out right and left.

Pisces: Then the fish swam in the floods.

Aries: The little ram, the time of little shoots and buds.

Taurus: The Bull, the great push of nature.

Gemini: The fertility of man. One seldom does better than twins.

Cancer: A drawback, the summer solstice. The crab walking backward when the sun descends again.

Leo: After the first inkling of solstice it dawns on man that the sun will really be going, from the 22nd of July till the 21st of August, just when all is most glowing.

Virgo: When man is roaring like a lion there is nothing better to tame him than a virgin. She will cut the hair of the lion and make it short, like Samson and Delilah. It is not nice, the whole symbolism is somewhat obscene. But at that time of the year, the 15th of September in the Egyptian calendar, the left eye of the goddess is prepared to receive the god Ra, who is to walk into it.[13] The eye is a womb symbol. The female element takes the lead. The god enters the womb of darkness. Yang is under Yin. Woman is on top.

Libra: The balance after the virgin has done her job.

Scorpio: The fatal self-sacrifice of the sun. The sun gets cornered by the virgin and when the forces are equal (Libra), the sun commits suicide, and then comes a clear descent into the mother. There is a legend that when the scorpion is surrounded by fire it kills itself.

Sagittarius: The death of the sun. Death is a sort of river or gap. There is a life beyond, but one is here on this bank of the river and cannot get there. Then comes the legend of the centaur, a good archer, who with his bow can send an arrow across. It is a means of communication. The archer Sagittarius with the arrow of intuition foresees new birth out of the unconscious. This is the advent season, when ghosts begin to walk again, when the unconscious begins to manifest itself.

Capricorn: The goat-fish. (This was the imperial sign on the coat-of-arms of Augustus Caesar.) After the dead man contained in the sea, the next sign is this goat-fish. He is half fish and half goat, meaning that at first, as the fish, he is deep down in the sea, out of sight in the unconscious. Then he rises to the surface and climbs to the highest peaks and valleys. This is the sun, the promise of the new year, so some astrologers call the time after Christmas the "Promise of the Year." It is the time of the birth of Mithras, the birth of Christ, the birth of the new light, the whole hope of the coming year. People born then have strong hearts. They are ambitious, but they have to work hard to achieve their ends.

But the new year has to be generated. The sun generates the year in Aquarius. Aquarius pours out the waters of fecundity. He is also a phallic god like Priapus.

After the generating water the Fishes come again, and so on around.

This is how the Zodiac came into existence. It is really a seasonal cycle with particular qualities of climate—winter, spring, summer, autumn, qualified by the fantasies and metaphorical imagination of the human mind. And so man has called the stars that are synchronous with the seasons by names expressing the qualities of each particular season. The active principle is obviously the time and not at all the stars, they are merely incidental. If, at the time when astrology came into conscious existence, other constellations had been in the heavens, we would have had different groups of stars but they would have been called a lion or a man carrying a water-jug just the same. They are not at all like their names, even the most striking constellations. It is a tremendous strain for the imagination.

Sun Symbolism

From: "7 June 1933," *Visions*

"A great heat went through me and when I lifted my foot I saw marked upon the sole, a Chinese dragon twined upon a cross, and above the cross the head of a lion."

Dr. Jung: Yes, the bristling mane of the lion symbolizes the rays of the sun, like the hair of Samson. And the lion astrologically is the *domicilium solis*,[14] it is the sign between the 21st of July and the 24th of August, when the sun is at its greatest power. So this lion can stand for this sun but in the particular aspect of the lion. For the sun, or whatever the sun means, can be symbolized in many different ways; if by the lion, it would mean power of a special kind, in the form of a powerful animal, not of a powerful man. The sun is also symbolized by the face of Moses, with the horns meaning radiation, therefore they would be the horns of power. And his face radiated such light when he came down from Sinai that only when it was veiled could the people gaze upon it; that would be the sun in the form of enlightened man. Also the sun is symbolized by the crown of Helios, the sun god, the radiation or the crown of sun rays which the old Caesars used to wear; one sees it chiefly on Roman coins. There the sun would express the human mind or understanding, or the human spirit, it would be a specifically human quality. But here the sun is in the form of the animal. How do you explain that?

Mr. Allemann: It is a symbol of fierce impulsive energy. Sekhmet represented the heat of the sun, and she also had a lion's head.

Dr. Jung: Yes, those of you who have been in Luxor remember that great statue of the goddess Sekhmet. It is made of the most beautiful black basalt, and she has the head of a lioness. She personified the terrible destructive power of Ra, or the sun at its height, at the hottest time of the year.

Horoscope, showing the houses, zodiac, and planets.
Source: Woodcut by Erhard Schoen for the nativity calendar of Leonhard Reymann (1515); reproduced from Jung's Collected Works, *Vol. 12.*

Mandalas, Birth Charts, and the Self

From: "Individual Dream Symbolism in Relation to Alchemy," (1936) *Psychology and Alchemy* (*CW* 12), par. 314

As to the interpretation [of a mandala] based on comparative historical material, we are in a more favourable position, at least as regards the general aspects of this figure. We have at our disposal, firstly, the whole mandala symbolism of three continents, and secondly, the specific time symbolism of the mandala as this developed under the influence of astrology, particularly in the West. The horoscope (see figure) is itself a mandala (a clock) with a dark centre, and leftward *circumambulatio* with "houses" and planetary phases. The mandalas of ecclesiastical art, particularly those on the floor before the high altar or beneath the transept, make frequent use of zodiacal beasts or the yearly seasons.

Astrology and Medicine

The topic of astrology and medicine is devoted to Jung's interest in the ideas of Paracelsus, the sixteenth century Swiss physician, alchemist, astrologer and natural philosopher. For Paracelsus, astrology was a source of critical knowledge for the physician, for without this knowledge one was not able to interpret the inner heaven or 'star of the body' correctly and thus effect healing for the patient. Jung writes, "There can be no doubt that Paracelsus was influenced by the Hermetic idea of 'heaven above, heaven below.' In his conception of the inner heaven he glimpsed an eternal primordial image, which was implanted in him and in all men, and recurs at all times and places. 'In every human being,' he says, 'there is a special heaven, whole and unbroken.'"[15]

From: "Paracelsus the Physician," (1942) *The Spirit in Man, Art and Literature* (*CW* 15), par. 22, 29-30

[Paracelsus] was mainly interested in the cosmic correlations, such as he found in the astrological tradition. His doctrine of the "star in the body" was a favourite idea of his, and it occurs everywhere in his writings. True to the conception of man as a microcosm, he located the "firmament" in man's body and called it the "astrum" or "Sydus." It was an endosomatic heaven, whose constellations did not coincide with the astronomical heaven but originated with the individual's nativity, the "ascendant" or horoscope.

The physician had to be not only an alchemist but also an astrologer,[16] for a second source of knowledge was the "firmament." In his *Labyrinthus medicorum* Paracelsus says that the stars in heaven must be "coupled together," and that the physician must "extract the judgment of the firmament from them."[17] Lacking this art of astrological interpretation, the physician is but a "pseudomedicus." The firmament is not merely the cosmic heaven, but a body which is a part or content of the human body. "Where the body is, there will the eagles gather. And where the medicine is, there do the physicians gather".[18] The firmamental body is the corporeal equivalent of the astrological heaven.[19] And since the astrological constellation makes a diagnosis possible, it also indicates the therapy. In this sense the firmament may be said to contain the "medicine." The physicians gather round the firmamental body like eagles round a carcass because, as Paracelsus says in a not very savoury comparison, "the carcass of the natural light" lies in the firmament. In other words, the *corpus sydereum* is the source of illumination by the *lumen naturae*, the "natural light," which plays the greatest possible role not only in the writings of Paracelsus but in the whole of his thought. This intuitive conception is, in my opinion, an achievement of the utmost historical importance, for which no one should grudge Paracelsus undying fame. It had a great influence on his contemporaries and an even greater one on the mystic thinkers who came afterwards, but its significance for philosophy in general and for the theory of knowledge in particular still lies dormant. Its full development is reserved for the future.

The physician should learn to know this inner heaven. "For if he knows heaven only externally, he remains an astronomer and an astrologer; but if he establishes its order in man, then he knows two heavens. Now these two give the physician knowledge of the part which the upper sphere influences. This [part?] must be present without infirmity in the physician in order that he may know the *Caudam Draconis* in man, and know the *Arietem* and *Axem Polarem*, and his *Lineam Meridionalem*, his Orient and his Occident." "From the external we learn to know the internal." "Thus there is in man a firmament as in heaven, but not of one piece; there are two. For the hand that divided light from darkness, and the hand that made heaven and earth, has done likewise in the microcosm below, having taken from above and enclosed within man's skin everything that heaven contains. For that reason the external heaven is a guide to the heaven within. Who, then, will be a physician who does not know the external heaven? For we live in this same heaven and it lies before our eyes, whereas the heaven within us is not before the eyes but behind them, and therefore we cannot see it. For who can see through the skin? No one.

Part III: Astrological Ages and the Precession of the Equinoxes

The world view that periods of time or aeons are ruled by certain principles that are related to the divine order of the cosmos and the gods, is a universal idea present in many cultures and religious traditions. The idea of astrological ages, or Platonic months, is one such idea from the western tradition originating in ancient Greece. It is based on the image of the twelve signs of the zodiac with their constellations forming a belt around the earth through which the sun appears to journey from our earthbound or geocentric perspective. The completion of a full cycle of the sun through the zodiac, called a Great or Platonic year, takes approximately 26,000 years to complete.

An astrological age is one twelfth of the Great Year, corresponding with the one zodiacal sign, therefore lasting approximately 2,200 years. It is calculated by assessing which zodiacal constellation hosts the sun at the time of the spring equinox (March 20). That the sign in which the spring point falls changes is due to what is called the precession of the equinoxes. The Earth's wobble on its axis causes the location of the sun to change zodiac signs at the spring point. Thus for the last 2,200 years the sun has been in the constellation of Pisces on the spring equinox point, hence the age of Pisces. As the sun moves into the next preceding sign of the zodiac, the age shifts to that of Aquarius.[20] We are currently in a period of great transition wherein the ruling principles are shifting.

Jung's interest in the astrological ages and the symbolic significance of the precession of the equinoxes has to do with the archetypal perspective that it affords to larger cycles of the collective. What he and others identified is how the religious symbolism of an era coincides with that of the astrological sign. As Alice O. Howell puts it, the zodiac in its Platonic cycle can be understood as "a marvellously slow moving clock that seems to describe the evolution of the Collective Unconscious, since each of these ages has an uncanny way of bringing forth a new spiritual movement or religion that by an odd synchronicity or coincidence uses in its method and symbols the very characteristic and symbols of the astrological constellation that it reflects".[22]

Jung's interest in the astrological ages provided him with a symbolic perspective on the shifting values and perspectives of the Christian era and modern life. The chapters that comprise this part of the book are taken mostly from *Aion*, Jung's later life work that focused on the psychology of Christianity and the Christ-symbol. While this figure compensated the collective consciousness of the early Christian phase, and represents the self or the movement to psychic completion, Jung argues that the Christ-symbol only does so partially because of his one-sided goodness and perfection. "The self is best represented by symbols that unite the opposites, while the Christ-symbol represents only one side, the other being shown by his enemy, the Antichrist or Satan."[22] The astrological age of Pisces, which is symbolized by the two fish, provided Jung with an archetypal ground for his views on the psychology of Christianity and the problem of the opposites when there is a splitting between good and evil. Jung wrote, "A synchronicity exists between the life of Christ and the objective astronomical event, the entrance of the spring equinox into the sign of Pisces. Christ is therefore the "Fish" . . . and comes forth as the ruler of the new aeon."[23] The resulting psychological task for modern individuation becomes the overcoming of this opposition. This is symbolized by the coming age of Aquarius whose zodiac sign is a human figure who pours water from a vase.

Astrological amplification helped Jung establish and deepen his psychological insights on the archetypal background to historical events. His interest in the synchronicity or coincidence between the religious ideas that grip the collective unconscious during the ruling astrological age and the insights afforded through astrological symbolism is illustrated in the selections that comprise these chapters.

Cycles and Spirals, Evolution and Involution

From: "14 June 1933," *Visions*

Dr. Jung: Here is a question by Miss Hannah: "You said last time that it was very questionable if there was any movement for the better in the world. What did you mean by better? I had thought that every platonic year the consciousness gained might be a little beyond the point reached by the era before. A spiral seems to make more sense than an endlessly repeated circle. Or does time lose its significance altogether in higher consciousness, so making the circle idea bearable?"

The first question is difficult to answer definitely as you can appreciate. There was a more or less temperamental remark—that it was rather questionable whether things would be better and better in every way. For what does one mean by "better"? If one calls it better when consciousness widens out and civilization increases, then I say we are moving towards an improved state of things, for it is very probable that civilization does increase with certain relapses from time to time. There have been cycles when things fall back into relative chaos, but then they picked up again. As a whole, if one compares the year 10,000 B.C. with the year 2000 A.D. one must say that there is a difference; things seem to be less primitive than they were then. And if one could compare, say, the year 5000 with 150,000 B.C. in central Europe, one would again mark a quite noticeable difference. So in that sense one could say things have become better. But in another sense that is most questionable. I don't know whether our life is happier than the life of the primitive man, whether life today is better than life in the Middle Ages. . . .

It is quite different now, however; when one hears of shooting somewhere, one knows the next minute it may be right at one's door because the world has been thrown into a general conflagration. . . . Formerly we jumped when something fell down in our room, but now we jump when a pistol goes off 5000 miles away. So in those respects it is quite doubtful whether things have become better. But if one takes the increase of civilization, the widening out of consciousness, for the real goal of mankind, if one says it is bad when things are unconscious and better when they become conscious, then things have become better, and it *is* a spiral, as far as we can judge of humanity.

But don't forget that we have very limited knowledge, we don't know whether these three months of the platonic year are not a mere episode. Taurus, Aries, and the Fishes are the three spring months, and we don't know what will happen in two signs from now, in about 2300 years, when we reach the equivalent of the winter solstice, the turning point. Whether that whole episode of the widening out of consciousness will not be something quite different, whether it will not then be an involution of consciousness, we simply do not know. This problem is linked up with our attitude to human things in general, namely, the question whether we have to think of the earthly life that we know empirically as the only life possible, or whether there is another form of existence, whether the goal of all things living is fulfilled by their existence here, or whether this is merely a means to an end.

The Coming Age of Aquarius

From: "On the Frontiers of Knowledge," *C.G. Jung Speaking* (1977), 398-99

You speak of a change of eras, of a new Platonic month, of the passage into another sign of the zodiac.[24] *What do you mean by that, what reality do such constellations have?*

People don't like you to talk about that, you will get yourself laughed at. Nobody has read Plato—you haven't either. Yet he is one of those who has come closest to the truth. The influence of the constellations, the zodiac, they exist; you cannot explain why, it's a "Just-So Story," that proves itself by a thousand signs. But men always go from one extreme to the other, either they don't believe, or they are credulous, any knowledge or faith can be ridiculed on the basis of what small minds do with it. That's stupid and, above all, it's dangerous. The great astrological periods do exist. Taurus and Gemini were prehistoric periods, we don't know much about them. But Aries the Ram is closer; Alexander the Great was one if its manifestations.[25] That was from 2000 B.C. to the beginning of the Christian era. With that era we came into the sign of the Fishes. It was not I who invented all the fish symbols there are in Christianity: the fisher of men, the *pisciculi christianorum*. Christianity has marked us deeply because it incarnates the symbols of the era so well. It goes wrong in so far as it believes itself to be the only truth; when what it is is one of the great expressions of truth in our time. To deny it would be to throw the baby out with the bathwater. What comes next? Aquarius, the Water-pourer, the falling of water from one place to another. And the little fish receiving the water from the pitcher of the Water-pourer, and whose principal star is Fomalhaut, which means the "fish's mouth." In our era the fish is the content; with the Water-pourer, he becomes the container. It's a very strange symbol. I don't dare interpret it. So far as one can tell, it is the image of a great man approaching. One finds, besides, a lot of things about this in the Bible itself: there are more things in the Bible than the theologians can admit.

It's a matter of experience that the symbolism changes from one sign to another, and there is the risk that this passage will be all the more difficult for the men of today and tomorrow because they no longer believe in it, no longer want to be conscious of it. Why when Pope Pius XII in one of his last discourses deplored that the world was no longer conscious enough of the presence of angels, he was saying to his faithful Catholics in Christian terms exactly what I am trying to say in terms of psychology to those who stand more chance of understanding this language than any other.

Endnotes

[1] *Jung on Astrology*, Eds. Safron Rossi and Keiron Le Grice. London, UK: Routledge, 2017.
[2] Jung, "Richard Wilhelm: In Memoriam" (1930) in *The Spirit in Man, Art, and Literature* (*CW* 15), 81.
[3] Jung, Letter to Sigmund Freud, 12 June 1911, in *Letters I*, 24.
[4] Greene, *Relating*, 53.
[5] Greene, *Relating*, 99.
[6] Howell, *Jungian Symbolism in Astrology*, 176.
[7] See Rossi, "Saturn in C. G. Jung's Liber Primus."
[8] Howell, *Jungian Symbolism in Astrology*, 6.
[9] Tarnas, *Cosmos and Psyche*, 69.
[10] Arroyo, *Astrology, Psychology, and the Four Elements,* 29.
[11] Stein, *Jung's Treatment of Christianity*, 154.
[12] Jung, "Part Two" (1912/52) in *Symbols of Transformation* (*CW* 5), par. 297.
[13] "It [the first day in autumn] is the day on which 'the goddess Nehmit completes her work, so that the god Osiris may enter the left eye.'"—Heinrich Brugsch, *Religion und Mythologie der alten Aegypter* (Leipzig, 1885), pp. 281ff, quoted in *Symbols of Transformation*, par. 408 (as in 1912 edn.).
[14] *Domicilium solis* translates as house of the sun. The sun rules Leo, the sign of the lion.

[15] Jung, "Paracelsus the Physician" (1942) in *The Spirit in Man, Art and Literature* (*CW* 15), par. 31.
[16] Paracelsus makes no real distinction between astronomy and astrology.
[17] Ch. II (Huser, I), p. 267.
[18] Ibid.
[19] *Paragranum*, p. 50: "As in the heavens so also in the body the stars float free, pure, and have an invisible influence, like the arcana."
[20] The topic of the precession of the equinoxes and the astrological ages is explained with succinct clarity by Alice O. Howell in *Jungian Symbolism Astrology*.
[21] Howell, *Jungian Symbolism in Astrology*, 23.
[22] Stein, *Jung's Treatment of Christianity*, 148.
[23] Jung, *Memories, Dreams, Reflections*, 220-221.
[24] "Flying Saucers: A Modern Myth," CW 10, par. 589.
[25] The Arabic name for Alexander was Dhulqarnein, "two-horned." Cf. *Symbols of Transformation*, CW 5, par. 283, n. 32, also Pl. XXa.

Bibliography

Arroyo, Stephen. *Astrology, Psychology, and the Four Elements.* Sebastopol, CA: CRCS, 1975.

Greene, Liz. *Relating: An Astrological Guide to Living with Others on a Small Planet.* York Beach, ME: Samuel Weiser, 1978.

Howell, Alice O. *Jungian Symbolism in Astrology.* Wheaton, Ill: A Quest Book, 1987.

Jung, Carl Gustav. *C. G. Jung Letters I: 1906-1950.* Edited by Gerald Adler and Aniela Jaffe. Trans. R. F. C. Hull. London: Routledge & Kegan Paul, 1973.

———. *C. G. Jung Speaking.* Edited by William McGuire and R. F. C. Hull. Princeton: Princeton University Press, 1977.

———. *Civilization in Transition.* 2nd ed. Vol. 10 of *The Collected Works of C. G. Jung.* Trans. R. F. C. Hull. Princeton: Princeton University Press, 1970.

———. *Dream Analysis: Notes on the Seminar Given in 1928-1930.* Bollingen Series XCIX. Edited by William McGuire. Princeton, NJ: Princeton University Press, 1984.

———. *Memories, Dreams, Reflections.* Edited by Aniela Jaffé. Trans. Richard and Clara Winston. New York, NY: Vintage Books, 1989.

———. *Psychology and Alchemy*, 2nd ed. Vol. 12 of *The Collected Works of C. G. Jung*. Trans. R. F. C. Hull. Princeton: Princeton University Press, 1968.

———. *The Spirit in Man, Art, and Literature*. Vol. 15 of *The Collected Works of C. G. Jung*. Trans. R. F. C. Hull. Repr. Princeton: Princeton University Press, 1966/1971.

———. *Symbols of Transformation*, 2nd ed. Vol. 5 of *The Collected Works of C. G. Jung*. Trans. R. F. C. Hull. Princeton: Princeton University Press, 1967.

———. *Visions: Notes of the Seminar Given in 1930-1934*. Edited by Claire Douglas. Princeton (Bollingen Series XCIX), 1997. 2 volumes.

Rossi, Safron. "Saturn in C.G. Jung's Liber Primus" in *Jung Journal: Culture & Psyche*, Volume 9, number 4. 38-57, 2015.

Stein, Murray. *Jung's Treatment of Christianity*. Wilmette, Ill: Chiron Publications, 1986.

Tarnas, Richard *Cosmos and Psyche: Intimations of a New World View*. New York: Viking, 2006.

Earthquake Prediction Model IV

By Jagdish Maheshri

ABSTRACT: The objective of this research was to further continue[1,2,3] analyzing and investigating correlations between astronomical data and earthquakes, with the intended goal of predicting future earthquakes with a greater advanced warning and higher degree of accuracy than current technology. Specifically, it focuses on severe earthquakes that occurred during the last century, with special emphasis on earthquakes of magnitude 7 or higher. This research work has already shown[1,2,3] a correlation between certain inter-planetary configurations (encompassing the relative geocentric positions and angles of all planets) and the occurrence of strong earthquakes. Building on the work done since the last publication[1,2,3], which focused on the validation of data employed from other resources[4] wherever possible and extending the data set to include the earthquakes of magnitude 7 or higher from January 1900 to December 2009, this research attempts to explore if any correlation exists between the declination angles of planets and the occurrence of strong earthquakes of magnitude 7 and higher. The previous work was based on the longitudinal geocentric angle between each planetary pair and included the Model I, the 15-degree multiple angles, the model II, the 12-degree multiple angles and the Model III, the top 16 most frequently occurred angles. This work extends the research by including the top 16 most frequently occurring declination angles for each planetary pair as well as sun's declination angles with every other planet model. As a result, between the two sets of Model IV, the sun-based declination angle model seems to predict earthquakes of magnitude 7 or higher with an order of magnitude better than the top 16 most frequently occurring declination angle model. However, compared to the Model III, the performance of both cases of Model IV was about two orders of magnitude poorer. Further research is necessary to build a useful, predictive model that can assess the probability of a given earthquake occurring during a certain time period at a given geographical location on earth. Predicting earthquakes well in advance of the state of the art will promote, protect, and enhance the world economy, potentially saving millions of lives.

Introduction

Although this paper focuses on earthquake prediction since 1993, the research began by studying the influence of planetary configurations on natural calamities in general. Starting in 2000, these predictions have been made available to the public on a monthly basis at www.astroinsight.com. While further research is warranted to include the place and type of natural disaster in the predictions, the time periods for the occurrences of natural disasters have been predicted in monthly columns[5]. Beginning in 2006, the research of the natural calamities was more focused on the occurrence of earthquakes. One reason for this was the availability of accurate data on earthquakes from National Earthquake Information Center, United States Geological Survey[6].

There is absolutely no precedent in predicting an earthquake solely based on planetary configuration. An occurrence of an earthquake is a random event and it can sometimes occur more frequently than other times. In 2006, this research began with the idea that planetary positions along the ecliptic and, therefore, their apparent (geocentric) positions as viewed from earth, may potentially correlate with the occurrence of earthquakes. Based on planetary characteristics and a large amount of earthquake data, several hypotheses were tested to see if these correlations actually exist. The results of this exercise indicated that certain planetary configurations seem to correlate reasonably well with earthquakes. This research has evolved from 15-degree multiple angles (Model I) to 12-degree multiple angles (Model II) and then to the top 16 most frequently occurring geocentric longitudinal angles (Model III). The intent of this paper is to highlight the initial findings of the next model (the model IV) on prediction of earthquakes based on the planetary declination angles.

A declination of a point (or planet) is the angular distance measured in the perpendicular direction north or south of the celestial equator. An angular distance measured along the north direction of the celestial equator is positive and the angular distance measured along the south direction is negative. Thus, when the declination of Mars is 22 degrees, its position is measured as 22 degrees with respect to the celestial equatorial plane (which is the same as the earth's equatorial plane extended in an infinite direction) along the arc perpendicular to the earth's equatorial plane. It is same as the latitude location on earth's surface except that it's on the celestial earth's sphere. Thus, Sun's declination on June 21 (summer solstice) is 23 degrees and 26 minutes and the same on December 21 (winter solstice). Similarly, it is zero on the days when the spring (March 21) and autumn (September 22/23) equinoxes occur as the Sun crosses the celestial equator on those days. It must be recognized that relative to the planets the Sun never moves; it is always fixed. But due to the earth's tilt and the diurnal rotation it appears to move. If the earth's north-south pole axis was not tilted the Sun declination would always be zero.

Sometimes the declination of a planet is referred to as declination angle, but mostly it is referred to as declination. In this paper it is either referred to as declination or declination position. Consider two planets, Jupiter and Venus.Let us say that Jupiter's declination position is 15 degrees north and Venus's declination position is 10 degrees south.an angle is typically formed by three points: two points give a straight line, and two straight lines meeting at a common point form an angle. Since the earth is in its equatorial plane, implicit in the definition of declination angle between Jupiter and Venus is the angle formed between the Jupiter-Earth arc and Venus-Earth arc measured along the perpendicular direction of the earth's equatorial plane.The declination angle between Jupiter and Venus is thus 25 degrees (Jupiter is 15 degrees on the north side of the Earth's equator and Venus is 10 degrees on south side of the earth's equator). In other words, a declination angle between two planets is the difference between their declination (angular difference) positions or the difference between their latitude positions on the celestial sphere. When two planets are said to be in parallel, they are at the same declination (position) and therefore, naturally, the declination angle between them is zero. For contraparallel planets the declination angle will be twice the declination of either planet.

Research Basis—Methodology

As pointed out earlier, the basis for this research is the unique planetary declination positions surrounding the earth. Astronomical data provides planetary declination positions as a function of time. It was observed that the declination angles of certain magnitudes between some pairs of planets with respect to Earth appear to correlate with earthquakes The hypothesis of this research is that the correlations between earthquakes of the past and their corresponding planetary declination angles during those respective periods occur in a statistically significant way.

The Model

The objective for this model development is to predict earthquakes of magnitude 7 and higher based on declination angles between planetary pairs. First a simple model was developed based on the assumption that the earthquake severity depends on the total number of angles ranging from zero to 54 degrees (note that a typical declination range is -23.5 to 23.5 degrees, giving a maximum of about a 47-degree declination angle; but with out-of-bounds planets the maximum angle can go as high as about 54 degrees) for the top 16 most frequently occurring declination angles for each pair of planets during 1900-2009 for seven and higher magnitude earthquakes. In other words, the more the number of angles the higher the severity of the earthquake. However, it was found that the severity of the earthquake is not necessarily proportional to the number of angles formed. As a result, it became necessary to account for the influence of each individual angle for each pair of planets by weighing them differently. The weighted model is developed using a simple linear regression technique. Thus, in theory there are 45 different pairs of planets (six outer, two inner, Sun, and Moon) and 16 distinct declination angles (from zero degrees to about 54 degrees), making a total of 720 maximum possible unique variables that can influence the earthquake occurrence. An orb of six minutes for each declination angle was employed for the analysis.

Since the Moon's average daily variation is about two declination degrees, it can form an almost equal number of angles with every other planet during a daily 24-hour period. Nonetheless, to test the influence of the Moon, two sets of models, one with the inclusion of Moon and the other without, were developed.

Earthquakes of magnitude 7 or higher that occurred between

January 1900 and December 2009 were obtained from the USGS[3,5] website. Two data sets of 1900-1972 and 1973-2009 were combined to create one large data set of 1672 points. To avoid the co-linearity in data employed, if there was more than one earthquake of magnitude 7 or higher occurring in one day, only the one with the highest magnitude was selected for that day for this analysis. The accuracy of the data sets was verified against the *Centennial Earthquake Catalog*[3]. The first step of the analysis was to determine the top 16 frequently occurring declination angles between 1900 and 2009. An example of the Neptune-Saturn pair is shown in Figure 1. The top 16 angles for this pair are: 2.6, 0.2, 2.3, 0.8, 10.2, ------- 8.6. And the corresponding frequency of the occurrences of these angles is: 34, 25, 23, 22, 19, -------14 respectively. Thus, for the Neptune-Saturn pair, the declination angle of 2.6 degrees occurred 34 times during 1900-2009 for earthquakes of 7 and higher magnitudes. Then computations of angles for all the 45 planetary angle pairs were performed. Using an orb of six minutes, the planetary data pertaining to the top 16 angles were extracted for all 45 planetary angle pairs for the model and are listed in Appendix A. Thus there are 720 unique variables. A linear model is assumed as follows.

Earthquake Magnitude = Σ Cn * (angle pair)n + constant for n = 1 to 720

where Cn is the coefficient of the nth angle pair; and the nth angle pair equals one when true and zero otherwise.

For example, Neptune-Saturn 2.6 declination angle is represented by the X_{161}^{th} variable which becomes unity only when the angle between Neptune and Saturn lies between 2.5 and 2.7 degrees. For all other angles between Neptune and Saturn, X_{161}^{th} variable equals zero.

A linear regression was performed and all the coefficients were estimated by generalized least squares. A number of coefficients were so small in magnitude that their influence on the

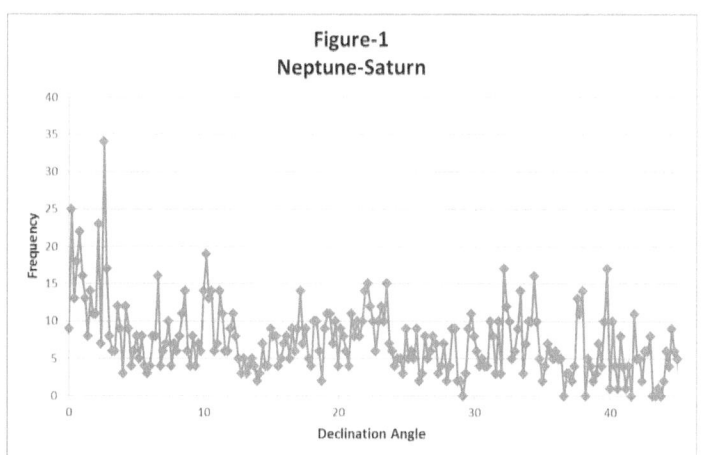

Figure-1
Neptune-Saturn

model was deemed negligible. The corresponding variables were omitted one at a time and the regression was repeated to confirm that their influence on the model was negligible. As mentioned earlier, two sets of models were developed, one with the inclusion of the Moon (referred to here as with-Moon model) and the other without Moon (referred here as without-Moon model). For each of these models, two cases were obtained as follows:

The first case includes all the variables (720 variables for with-Moon model and 576 variables for without-Moon model).

The second case where the insignificant variables were omitted subject to the criteria of t>=1, where "t" is the statistical test that measures the significance of the coefficient. For this case there were 308 variables for the with-Moon model and 244 variables for the without-Moon model.

A typical set of coefficients of model variables are shown in Table-1 for the 308-variable with-Moon model. There are 45 rows representing planetary pairs and 16 columns for the corresponding angles. Naming of the planetary pairs employs the characters Pl, Ne, Ur, Sa, Ju, Mr, Ve, Mc and Su for Pluto, Neptune, Uranus, Saturn, Jupiter, Mars, Venus, Mercury and

Table-1
308 Variables with Moon Model

Angle #-> Angle Pair	1	2	3	4	5	6	7	8	9	10	11	12	13	14	15	16
Pl-Ne	0.197	0.2728			-0.173	-0.158	0.1307			-0.091	0.1318	0.1163				
Pl-Ur			-0.08			0.1839	-0.071		-0.074		-0.091	0.1114				0.354
Pl-Sa			-0.155			-0.111		0.2795		-0.075	-0.195				-0.101	-0.239
Pl-Ju				0.1631	0.1028	0.095		-0.108			0.1332	-0.169		0.1251		
Pl-Mr	0.0709							0.06			0.2935	-0.114	0.2173		0.1898	0.1559
Pl-Ve		0.207	0.3603	0.1517	0.092			0.3127			0.1349	0.1697	-0.298	-0.245		
Pl-Mc	0.1525		0.0897					-0.1	-0.285	-0.183	-0.125	0.3508			0.3369	
Pl-Su			0.1894	-0.085	0.1145	-0.111	-0.104	0.243				-0.129	-0.105		-0.155	-0.163
Pl-Mn	0.1337			0.1066		-0.152				0.1994	0.217	-0.145			-0.157	
Ne-Ur	-0.113		0.108	-0.084	0.1888	-0.11	-0.212	-0.132	0.2977					-0.106	-0.197	
Ne-Sa						-0.118	0.5011	-0.184		0.3023			-0.169	-0.226		0.0741
Ne-Ju			0.1748	-0.137		0.245					0.2336	-0.167	0.1903	0.2001	-0.146	
Ne-Mr			0.0973	0.0937	-0.147	0.1383		0.1029			0.0772	0.2292			-0.091	
Ne-Ve							-0.222			-0.098		0.2185		0.1997		
Ne-Mc	-0.108			-0.113	-0.106		0.1769	-0.173				0.2691			-0.193	0.165
Ne-Su		0.0716	0.1112	-0.115	-0.112		-0.085			0.0968			0.1147			-0.126
Ne-Mn		-0.148	-0.108		0.125	-0.223		-0.186			-0.129				-0.089	-0.219
Ur-Sa	0.0786	0.0784		-0.149							-0.094		-0.132	0.0876		
Ur-Ju					0.1791	0.1558					-0.191	-0.135	-0.098	-0.137		
Ur-Mr		-0.19	0.1112	0.1355						0.1			0.217			
Ur-Ve		-0.181	-0.1		-0.25	-0.102	-0.135				-0.144	-0.387	0.227	0.1803	0.1758	0.4025
Ur-Mc			0.1731			-0.152						-0.181			-0.141	
Ur-Su			0.1173						-0.127	0.1836			0.1532	-0.138		-0.241
Ur-Mn	-0.147	-0.079	-0.125	0.1205	-0.11		0.0706	-0.154	-0.171		-0.081	-0.104			0.1167	
Sa-Ju			0.1473				-0.071	0.1752	-0.1			-0.17	-0.124		-0.192	0.1404
Sa-Mr				0.1097		0.1212			0.1165			0.1418	0.1021		-0.104	
Sa-Ve	0.1904	0.1034	-0.175					-0.108	-0.173			0.0989	0.2225	0.1671	0.0986	
Sa-Mc		-0.371				0.3759	0.1522	-0.149		0.0809	0.1304			0.1108		0.1014
Sa-Su				-0.151	-0.089		-0.225	0.149	0.0906	-0.218		0.1432			-0.093	
Sa-Mn				0.163								0.1251	0.2042			-0.133
Ju-Mr		0.1403								0.1444						0.2406
Ju-Ve										-0.124	0.2289		-0.246	-0.122	-0.16	
Ju-Mc			-0.132				0.1604	-0.095			-0.092					
Ju-Sun					0.1719	-0.195			0.1364		-0.101			0.1148	-0.099	
Ju-Mn	-0.115			0.1178	0.2917	-0.284				0.2438	0.1293		0.1494	-0.124		
Mr-Ve		0.2488								0.199			0.1975			
Mr-Mc				0.3091		-0.143	-0.213		-0.14	-0.14	-0.113	-0.219		0.0975		
Mr-Su		-0.143	0.1112	-0.109	0.0704	0.1225	-0.107		0.2796		-0.092		-0.09			-0.198
Mr-Mn										-0.187		0.0712				
Ve-Mc	0.156	0.0785			0.0905			0.137				-0.227			0.259	0.131
Ve-Su			-0.061								0.073	0.1683				-0.089
Vn-Mn		0.1401					0.1438	-0.104	0.0772				0.1488	0.1245		
Mc-Su	-0.066	0.078	0.0867	-0.076			-0.067						-0.153			
Mc-Mn			0.1253	-0.15				-0.111		-0.124	-0.133	-0.097	0.279	0.1041		
Su-Mn		-0.127						0.1098		-0.085		-0.165		-0.296	0.1225	

Sun, respectively. Thus, Pl-Ne represents the planetary pair Pluto and Neptune, and Sa-Mc represents the planetary pair Saturn and Mercury.

The value of the constant in the linear equation of these models as calculated by robust linear regression ranged between 7.23 and 7.27. The simulation results showed that the first two models were almost identical in their performance as the successive omission of coefficients of insignificant magnitude did not seem to degrade the model performance while allowing the data noise reduction. The simulated results along with the actual earthquakes are shown in Figure 2 for these models, and although not included in the figure due to space limitations, a similar trend exists for all 1672 data points for each model.

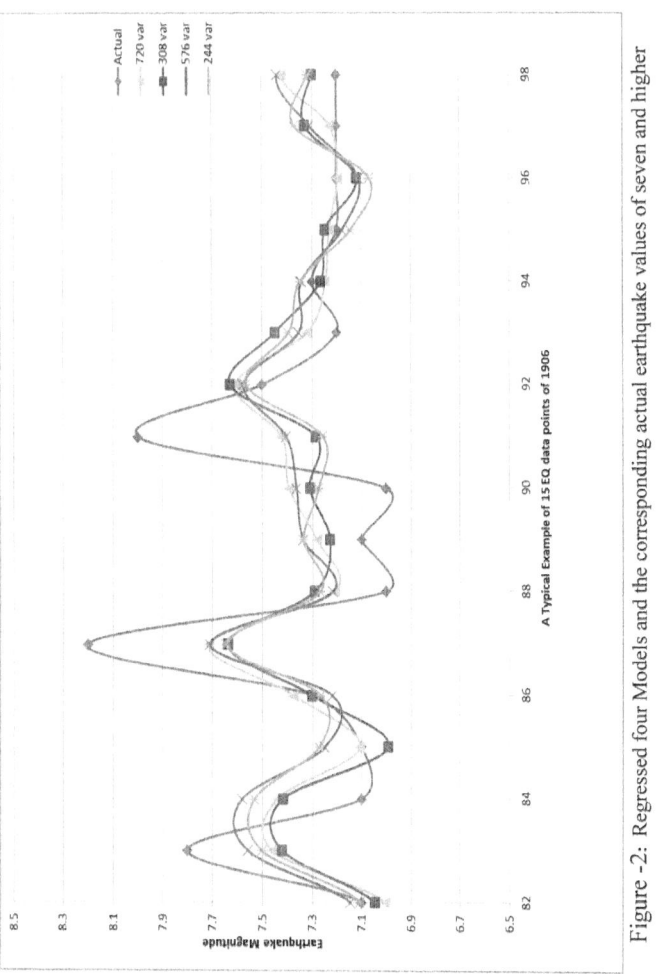

Figure -2: Regressed four Models and the corresponding actual earthquake values of seven and higher

It must be noted that one of the limitations of these models is that they only apply over a narrow range of seven and higher earthquake magnitude. Therefore, all predicted values for earthquakes below magnitude seven are irrelevant and meaningless since they can be applicable for the entire lower range of earthquake magnitudes from zero to 6.9. The other important limitation to these models is that they are based on only 1672 data points (since earthquakes of magnitude seven and higher occur about a dozen time per year). Thus, for example, for the model of 308 variables, the ratio of data points to model variables is just above five, and for the one with 244-variable model it is about 7. Consequently, the R-square term, which is a measure of a model fit, varied with decreasing amount of variables from 0.43 to 0.31 indicating a fit not so perfect.

Using Greenwich noontime daily planetary positions, each model was then used to predict the earthquakes for the year 2011-2014. A summary of assumptions reflecting the limitations described above form the basis for the models and are listed below:

1.The predicted earthquakes of magnitude less than 7 are ignored since the model is based on the earthquake data set of magnitude 7 and higher. Thus, the prediction dates of an earthquake of magnitude less than 7 also apply for the dates when earthquake did not occur.

2. As pointed out earlier, in order to determine the influence of angles made by Moon with other planets, two sets of models, with-Moon and the without-Moon were developed. The determination of the angles used for each pair of planets was based on the top 16 most frequently occurred declination angles for earthquakes of seven and higher magnitude during 1900-2009. Thus for each pair of planets, a unique set of 16 declination angles were used in the models.

3. After testing several different orbs for declination angles, a six minute (1/10th of a degree) orb is found to be most satisfactory, and therefore applied for all declination angles.

4. Since the predictions (or simulations) were computed on a daily basis corresponding to Greenwich noon, prediction is assumed to apply for the entire date (12 a.m. to the next 12 a.m. of Greenwich Time).

5. The minimum number of declination angles required to meet the criteria of realizing the earthquake of magnitude seven or higher must be higher than the daily average number of angles for that year.

6. The models thus obtained when applied to the daily Greenwich Noon declination angles for planets from the year 2011 to 2014 for earthquake predictions, the predicted resulted seem to overestimate the actual earthquakes about by the amount of their corresponding root mean square errors. Therefore, the predictions were corrected with the root mean square errors which ranged from 0.296 to 0.33.

Although the linear regression was performed using top 16 most frequently appeared declination angles for each planetary angle pair as independent variables, while setting up the equations for each 1672 earthquake data points of magnitude 7 and higher, a care was taken to omit the angle pair (a rare case) if it was not truly independent. For example, consider two planetary pairs: Saturn-Mars and Saturn-Venus. If the declination angle between Saturn and Mars is 10 degrees (as one of the 16 most frequent angles) and the declination angle between the Saturn and Venus is 15 degrees (also as one of the 16 most frequent angles) then the declination angle variable Mars-Venus is omitted if it's either 5 or 25 degrees as one of the top 16 most frequently occurred angles. It is important to note that the 45 declination angle pairs are based declination position of ten planets. However, because only top 16 declination angles for each pair are considered in the regression analysis, it is possible to have up to 720 (45 times 16) independent variables for all 1672 data points.

Alternatively another hypothesis is formulated with the assumption that the planetary declination angle pairs are based on a one common planet. Thus, for example, if Sun is assumed as a common planet then only the nine planetary declination angle pairs: Sun-Pluto, Sun-Neptune, Sun-Uranus,

Sun-Saturn, Sun-Jupiter, Sun-Mars, Sun-Venus, Sun-Mercury and Sun-Moon are considered.

In order to compare this hypothesis against the top 16 frequently occurred declination angles for each of 45 planetary pairs, as before, a linear regression was performed for each common planet case (nine planetary pairs for each common planet case) with top 80 frequently occurred declination angles. The top 80 angles were chosen to have the same total number of 720 variables for comparison. The results showing the R-square term, which is a measure of model fit, are listed in Table 2.

Table 2

Top 80 Declination Angles Models	R2 Term
Pluto based	0.4230
Neptune based	0.4361
Uranus based	0.4177
Saturn based	0.4384
Jupiter based	0.3973
Mars based	0.4395
Venus based	0.4290
Mercury based	0.4427
Sun based	0.4589
Moon based	0.4489

As shown in Table 2, the Sun based model has the highest value of the R-square term, and therefore, the best possible fit Sun based model is chosen for the analysis. The top 80 most frequently occurred declination angles for Sun based model pairs are listed in Appendix B. The linear regression analysis estimated all the variable coefficients by using generalized least square method. As with the previous model, two sets of models were developed, one with inclusion of Moon (all variables) and the other without Moon. In each of these sets, a number of variables (with very small value of coefficient) were omitted one at a time and the regression was repeated to confirm the influence of the omitted variables was indeed negligible. Thus for each of these two sets two cases were obtained as follows:

The first case includes all 706 variables (note that Sun-Mercury pair only had 66 total angles) for with-Moon model and 626 variables for without-Moon model.

The second case where the insignificant variables were omitted subject to the criteria of t>=1 where "t" is statistical test that measures the significance of the coefficient. For this case there were 344 variables for with-Moon model and 279 variables for without-Moon model.

A typical set of coefficients of model variables are shown in Table 3 for the 626-variable without-Moon model. There are eight columns representing planetary pairs and 80 rows for the corresponding angles. As before, naming of the planetary pairs employ characters Pl, Ne, Ur, Sa, Ju, Mr, Ve, Mc and Su for Pluto, Neptune, Uranus, Saturn, Jupiter, Mars, Venus, Mercury and Sun respectively. Thus, Pl-Su represents the planetary pair Pluto and Sun, and Sa-Su represents the planetary pair Saturn and Sun.

The value of the constant in the linear equation of these models as calculated by robust linear regression ranged between 7.13 and 7.30. The simulation results showed that the first two models for each case were almost identical in their performance as the successive omission of coefficients of insignificant magnitude did not seem to degrade the model performance while allowing the data noise reduction. The simulated results along with the actual earthquakes are shown in Figure 3 for these four models, and although not included in the figure due to space limitation, a similar trend exists for all 1672 data points for each model.

Table-3

626 Variables Coefficients for Sun based without Moon Model

Angle Pair-->	Pl-Su	Ne-Su	Ur-Su	Sa-Su	Ju-Sun	Mr-Su	Ve-Su	Mc-Su
Angle #								
1	-0.198	0.0988	-0.028	-0.002	-0.086	-0.003	0.0421	-0.031
2	0.1097	0.0045	-0.13	-0.005	0.0054	-0.128	0.0055	0.1779
3	0.0564	0.0817	-0.119	-0.047	-0.124	-0.018	0.0209	0.0679
4	-0.086	-0.102	-0.074	0.0669	-0.089	-0.166	-0.036	-0.016
5	0.1389	-0.011	-0.097	-0.101	0.1226	0.0523	0.0617	0.1115
6	-0.055	-0.022	0.0029	0.0296	-0.019	0.0788	-0.028	0.0743
7	-0.05	-0.034	0.1031	-0.333	0.1644	-0.029	0.0162	0.017
8	0.2786	-0.166	-0.012	0.0422	-0.164	0.0672	0.0325	-0.009
9	0.0395	0.0125	-0.079	0.1054	-0.02	0.2319	-0.001	-0.008
10	-0.062	-0.042	0.1274	-0.087	-0.021	0.0363	-0.017	0.008
11	-0.13	0.0616	-0.081	0.1371	-0.1	-0.21	0.0252	0.116
12	-0.087	-0.024	0.0978	0.1069	0.0732	-0.098	0.1205	0.0421
13	-0.023	0.0085	0.0218	-0.044	-0.068	-0.163	0.0628	0.0593
14	-0.128	0.0347	-0.059	-0.025	0.0369	0.0037	-0.02	-0.035
15	-0.15	-0.036	-0.065	-0.044	-0.191	0.0098	-0.051	0.0177
16	-0.107	-0.126	-0.161	0.0781	0.0027	-0.144	-0.155	0.0433
17	0.0686	0.0084	-0.02	-0.166	0.1359	-0.04	0.1619	-0.052
18	-0.037	0.0748	0.0063	0.0119	-0.131	-0.091	0.241	0.0399
19	0.0179	0.0499	-0.003	-0.079	-0.053	0.1049	0.1088	0.0904
20	-0.082	-0.124	-0.101	0.001	-0.006	-0.03	0.0326	0.0167
21	0.0259	-0.128	0.2144	0.1996	-0.128	-0.023	-0.046	-0.06
22	0.1427	-0.066	-0.244	-0.139	-0.011	-0.025	-0.125	0.0143
23	-0.007	-0.158	-0.032	-0.132	0.101	-0.09	0.0115	0.028
24	0.1391	0.0195	-0.092	-0.016	-0.12	0.1051	0.0556	0.1236
25	-0.073	0.13	0.1643	-0.09	0.0351	0.0058	0.0043	-0.094
26	0.1895	-0.071	-0.119	-0.161	-0.23	0.0531	0.0987	0.0685
27	0.0417	0.2122	0.0504	0.1176	-0.069	-0.165	-0.174	0.0276
28	0.0436	0.1148	0.0426	-0.129	0.1424	-0.074	0.0065	-0.011
29	-0.08	0.1045	-0.039	0.1216	-0.054	0.0041	0.0642	0.0103
30	0.0705	-0.172	-0.113	-0.173	-0.017	-0.004	0.0718	0.0644
31	-0.088	0.1849	0.0515	0.0323	-0.013	0.027	-0.111	-0.01
32	0.1887	-0.098	0.0062	0.2461	0.0913	-0.059	-0.049	-0.022
33	-0.121	0.2057	0.0097	0.0736	-0.053	0.2845	-0.037	0.0564
34	-0.254	-0.122	0.0215	0.0098	-0.099	-0.055	-0.035	-0.032
35	0.204	-0.107	0.0772	0.1454	-0.138	-0.252	-0.138	0.1957
36	-0.057	-0.079	-0.061	-0.012	0.0548	-0.079	-0.15	-0.003
37	0.0445	0.1513	-0.105	0.0811	-0.15	-0.068	-0.094	-0.122
38	-0.189	-0.09	-0.02	0.0241	-0.019	-0.094	-0.108	0.036
39	-0.098	-0.331	-0.058	0.1198	-0.092	0.2836	-0.027	0.1806
40	0.1456	0.0783	-0.141	-0.019	0.0326	0.1224	-0.126	0.1485

Table-3 (continue)

626 Variables Coefficients for Sun based without Moon Model

Angle Pair--> Angle #	Pl-Su	Ne-Su	Ur-Su	Sa-Su	Ju-Sun	Mr-Su	Ve-Su	Mc-Su
41	-0.209	0.0254	0.1278	-0.034	-0.109	-0.108	-0.035	0.1423
42	-0.014	0.035	0.1691	-0.166	-0.042	0.0544	0.1327	-0.077
43	0.0087	-0.07	0.1881	0.1004	-0.183	0.0684	0.1363	-0.023
44	-0.029	0.1861	0.0365	0.1293	-0.122	-0.034	0.0138	0.2996
45	0.1482	-0.119	-0.006	-0.015	-0.018	-0.028	-0.158	-0.038
46	0.1378	-0.155	-0.117	0.0021	0.1844	0.0281	0.0286	0.1466
47	0.0951	-0.142	0.2115	-0.158	-0.021	-0.039	-0.092	0.1074
48	-0.122	-0.042	0.1697	0.1262	-0.27	-0.153	0.0515	0.0588
49	-0.039	0.0332	0.0687	0.1278	-0.161	0.1103	0.1575	-0.117
50	-0.233	0.1437	-0.029	0.1012	0.1977	0.1052	0.0489	0.027
51	-0.171	0.0384	-0.172	0.3057	-0.139	0.0569	-0.004	0.1661
52	0.0149	0.003	-0.106	0.0701	-0.148	0.1199	0.0401	0.0438
53	-0.005	0.0443	0.0372	-0.041	0.1402	-0.001	0.0127	0.1565
54	-0.035	0.1867	-0.028	0.0917	0.0004	0.1032	0.0005	0.0656
55	-0.004	-0.084	-0.055	0.3696	0.118	-0.105	0.0153	0.0758
56	-0.239	-0.23	0.0434	-0.077	0.1954	-0.011	0.0047	0.0185
57	-0.02	-0.139	0.1183	-0.154	-0.114	-0.027	-0.154	-0.17
58	0.0823	-0.051	-0.064	-0.001	0.361	0.15	-0.323	0.2512
59	-0.043	0.1748	-0.041	-0.021	0.0823	-0.005	-0.045	0.0314
60	0.0287	-7E-04	0.15	-0.104	-0.052	-0.009	-0.183	-0.043
61	-0.244	-0.068	0.0719	0.0426	-0.051	0.3361	-0.115	0.1631
62	0.164	0.1842	-0.101	-0.029	-0.055	0.3235	-0.105	-0.267
63	0.0832	-0.057	0.0553	0.0333	-0.045	-0.015	0.0057	0.0806
64	-0.074	0.2044	0.0885	0.2698	-0.044	-0.052	-0.066	0.1779
65	0.0821	0.157	0.014	0.0257	0.0825	-0.039	-0.189	
66	-0.157	-0.09	-0.037	0.1177	-0.101	-0.347	-0.209	-0.142
67	-0.069	0.0473	0.2339	0.1718	0.0937	0.2787	0.0061	-0.158
68	-0.044	-0.065	-0.088	-0.13	0.0541	-0.078	0.0715	
69	-0.299	-0.126	0.259	0.0069	-0.075	-0.148	0.023	
70	-0.138	-0.003	0.2856	0.0249	-0.127	-0.122	-0.141	
71	0.0723	0.082	-0.276	0.1373	0.0392	-0.192	-0.188	
72	-0.104	0.2363	-0.106	0.11	-0.065	-0.106	0.0345	
73	0.2283	-0.121	0.0077	0.1318	0.038	-0.26	-0.234	
74	0.1461	0.0153	0.4549	0.2325	-0.228	-0.317	-0.097	
75	-0.028	-0.117	0.1146	0.0578	-0.012	-0.116	-0.166	
76	0.0263	-0.305	0.0935	0.2588	0.0821	-0.013	0.1909	
77	0.3455	0.2034	0.0636	-0.135	0.0483	-0.114	-0.246	
78	-0.015	0.0836	-0.169	-0.094	0.0081	0.1718	0.0014	
79	0.5399	-0.08	0.0272	-0.084	-0.027	-0.1	-0.018	
80	0.2109	-0.089	0.2034	-0.06	0.0715	-0.103	-0.041	

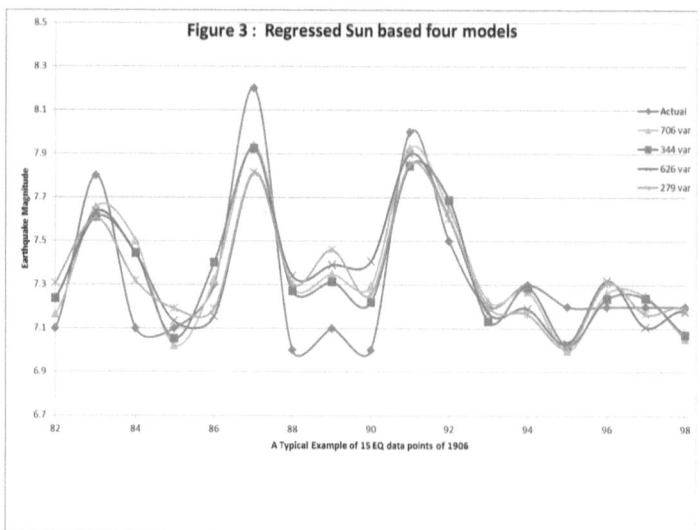

Using Greenwich noontime daily planetary positions, each sun based model was then used to predict the earthquakes for the year 2011-2014. As for the top 16 most frequently observed angles for each planetary pair model, a summary of assumptions reflecting the limitations described above for the Sun based top 80 frequently observed declination angles form the basis for the models and are listed below:

1. The predicted earthquakes of magnitude less than 7 are ignored since the model is based on the earthquake data set of magnitude 7 and higher. Thus, the prediction dates of an earthquake of magnitude less than 7 also apply for the dates when earthquake did not occur.

2. As pointed out earlier, in order to determine the influence of angles made by Moon with Sun, two sets of models, with-Moon and the without-Moon were developed. The determination of the angles used for each planet with Sun was based

on the top 80 most frequently occurred declination angles for earthquakes of seven and higher magnitude during 1900-2009. Thus for each pair of planet with Sun as a common planet, a unique set of 80 declination angles (except of Mercury-Sun only had 66 declination angles) were used in the models.

3. After testing several different orbs for declination angles, a six minute (1/10th of a degree) orb is found to be most satisfactory, and therefore applied for all declination angles.

4. Since the predictions (or simulations) were computed on a daily basis corresponding to Greenwich noon, prediction is assumed to apply for the entire date (12 a.m. to the next 12 a.m. of Greenwich Time).

5. The minimum number of declination angles required to meet the criteria of realizing the earthquake of magnitude seven or higher must be higher than the daily average number of angles for that year.

6. The models thus obtained when applied to the daily Greenwich Noon declination angles for planets from the year 2011 to 2014 for earthquake predictions, the predicted resulted seem to overestimate the actual earthquakes about by the amount of their corresponding root mean square errors. Therefore, the predictions were corrected with the root mean square errors which ranged from 0.289 to 0.319.

7. It must be noted that the model assumes the dependency on the angles of the planetary pairs with sun as a common planet in those pairs.

Results

As described above, this paper presents Model IV as two separate models, based on declination angle between each planetary pair. The first, the top 16 most frequently occurred declination angles for each one of the 45 planetary pairs for earthquakes of magnitude seven and higher during 1900-2009, and the second one, for the same period during which

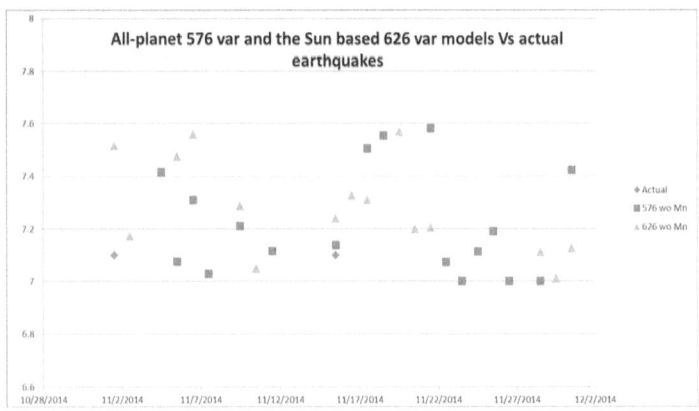

Figure 4. Comparison of 576 top 16 all-planet based and top 80 sun-based variable models predictions and the actual earthquake data for November 2014.

the earthquakes of magnitude seven and higher occurred, is the top 80 most frequently occurred declination angles for each one of the 9 Sun based planetary pairs with Sun as a common planet in every pair. These models will be referred here as Top 16 all-planet based and the top 80 sun based models. Furthermore each one of these two models there are two sets: with Moon and without Moon model, and each of these four sets have two cases each.

Both models, with two different set each, were tested to predict earthquakes of seven and higher magnitude for the period 2011-2014. For each one of these two models, the best results are provided by the 576 variable no-Moon top 16 all planet based model and the 626 variable no-Moon top 80 sun based model. The dates predicted by these models and the corresponding actual dates on which earthquakes occurred are shown in Figure 4 and are summarized in Table-4 for 2011-2014.

Figure 4 shows that out of the two earthquakes of magnitude 7 and higher that occurred in November 2014, the 576-variable

Table 4

2011 Months	Model III Prediction Dates	Actual Dates	Model IV (576 Var) Top 16 all planet based Prediction Dates	Model IV (626 Var) Top 80 Sun based Prediction Dates
Jan-11	1-6, 12-13, 15-20, 22, 28	1 (7), **2**(7.2), **13** (7), 18 (7.2)	1-4, 6, 8-12, 14, 16, 18-19, 21-22, 24, 26, 30-31	14-15, 17-18, 22, 24-26, 29-31
Feb-11	1, 6, 8, 14, 16-18, 21-22	None	2, 4, 7, 9, 11-12, 15, 27	2, 4, 9, 12, 17-19, 23
Mar-11	1, 6-8, 11-12, 15, 17-18, 21,26	9 (7.3), 11(9) Japan	1, 4-5, 9-23, 25, 30	2, 6-9, 15, 18-19, 22, 27, 31
Apr-11	7-9, 14, 25-26	7 (7.1)	9, 11, 15, 18, 26, 27, 30	2, 6, 15, 17, 30
May-11	1, 3-6, 10, 12, 20-21	None	8, 18, 19	13-14, 18-19
Jun-11	4-7, 10-13, 16, 24, 25, 27	24 (7.3)	4, 5, 21, 25-26, 29	None
Jul-11	4-7, 10, 13, 15, 19, 21-22, 28, 31	6 (7.6), 10 (7)	1, 3	None
Aug-11	7, 9, 15, 23-25, 27, 29-30	**20** (7.2), **24** (7)	9, 17, 19-20, 23-24, 27	1, 9, 11, 13, 20-21, 23-24
Sep-11	3, 14-15, 18-19, 24, 28	**3** (7), **15** (7.3)	11-12, 21, 26-28	1, 16

Months	Model III Prediction Dates	Actual Dates	Model IV (576 Var) Top 16 all planet based Prediction Dates	Model IV (626 Var) Top 80 Sun based Prediction Dates
Oct-11	11, 14-15, 24, 31	21(7.6), **23**(7.3)	2-3, 5-6, 9-11, 13-14, 17-20, 23-24, 26, 27, 30	3, 9, 11-12, 18-20, 31
Nov-11	6, 10, 14-16, 21-25, 27	None	1, 5, **8**, 10, 13-14, 20-21, 24, 30	2, 19
Dec-11	1, 5, *13-16*, 18, 21, 23-26, 31	14(7.3)	8, 17, 21	1, 26-27

2012

Months	Prediction Dates	Actual Dates	Prediction Dates	Prediction Dates
Jan-12	1, 5, 27 and 30	**10**(7.2)	7, 22, 25, 28	12, 15, 18, 21, 28-29
Feb-12	1, 9-10, 14, 17-18, 22-23, 27	2 (7.1)	3-5, 14	1, 4, 6, 10, 14, 16, 18, 21-22, 24, 26
Mar-12	1, 7-8, 13, 15-16, 18, 20-21, 26, 28-31	20(7.4), 25(7.1)	25	1, 7, 14, 19, 22, 23
Apr-12	21-22 and 26-27	**11**(8.6), 12(7)	None	3, 7, 9, *11*, 13-14, 17, 25
May-12	1, 5 and 19-20	None	20	3, 10, 13, 15
Jun-12	7, 21-22 and 28-29	None	3, 6, 18, 21	1
Jul-12	2, 10-12, 19, 21, 23-24 and 26	None	23, 26	3-4, 13, 28

Months	Prediction Dates	Actual Dates	Model IV (576 Var) Top 16 all planet based Prediction Dates	Model IV (626 Var) Top 80 Sun based Prediction Dates
Aug-12	9-12, 20-23, 27-29	14(7.7), 27(7.3), 31(7.6)	9	2, 4, 6, 9, 15, 25, 27, 29
Sep-12	11, 14-16, 19, 27, 30	5(7.6), 30(7.3)	21, 23, 27	6, 8
Oct-12	1-6, 9, 12-13, 16-17, 19-22, 24-26, 28, 30	28(7.8)	21, 26,	1, 3, 5-8, 13, 16-17, 25, 28, 30
Nov-12	2-5, 7, 16, 22, 24, 30	7(7.4)	14, 16, 22, 26-27	2-5, 8, 13-14, 15, 22, 25-26
Dec-12	1, 7, 13, 20, 23, 25-27	7(7.3), 10(7.1)	3, 5-6, 8-10, 13-14, 18, 20, 23, 28-31	8-9, 14, 18, 25, 27-28

2013	Model III			Model IV (576 Var) Top 16 all planet based Prediction Dates	Model IV (626 Var) Top 80 Sun based Prediction Dates
Months	Prediction Dates		Actual Dates		
Jan-13	1, 3-5, 8, 13-15, 22-25, 28-29		5(7.5)	2-3, 5-20, 22-23, 25, 27-28, 31	4, 9-10, 12, 14, 16-22, 26, 25-28
Feb-13	2, 10-13, 15, 18,		6(8), 8(7.1)	1, 4-5, 8-10, 13, 16-17, 24	2-3, 7-13, 16-18, 20-22, 25-28
Mar-13	1, 7, 10-13, 16-19, 21, 30-31		None	5, 21, 24, 28	8-9, 11-12, 14-15, 18-19, 21, 26, 28, 30-31

Month				
Apr-13	5, 8-9, 13-14, 16, 20-21, 25-28, 30	6(7), 16(7.7), 19(7.2)	1, 3, 12, 14-15, 19-20, 22	8-9, 11, 19, 26, 28-30
May-13	1-2, 4, 6-7, 12, 16-18, 20, 23, 29-30	23(7.4), 24(8.3)	11-12, 15-23, 26-27	4, 8, 11-13, 17, 20, 24-26, 28, 31
Jun-13	1, 3, 14, 16, 19, 22-24, 27, 30	None	2-4, 7-8, 11, 15, 18, 20, 25	4-6, 11-13, 27-29
Jul-13	1, 4-5, 7-8, 12-13, 15, 17-19, 23	7(7.3), 15(7.3)	3, 6-9, 11-12, 20-21, 23, 25	6-7, 12, 15-16, 20, 24, 28, 31
Aug-13	1-6, 10, 12, 14, 18, 22, 29-30	30(7)	1, 28	1-2, 9, 16, 23-25
Sep-13	2, 8, 15, 18, 21, 23, 26-28,	24(7.7), 25(7.1)	1-4	4, 5, 7, 14, 16, 24
Oct-13	1, 3, 6-8, 10-13, 16-19, 22, 26, 28, 30-31	15(7.1), 25(7.1)	19	1, 5, 8-10, 12, 14-16, 20, 22-23, 26, 29
Nov-13	3, 7-9, 11-13, 15-18, 23, 25-28	17(7.7), 25(7)	4, 5	2-4, 7, 10, 12-13, 15, 17-19, 23, 28-29
Dec-13	6, 14, 16-17, 20-22, 25-26, 28-29	None	1, 6-7, 9-10, 14, 17, 21, 30-31	3, 5-6, 8, 16, 21

2014 Months	Model III Prediction Dates	Actual Dates	Model IV (576 Var) Top 16 all planet based Prediction Dates	Model IV (626 Var) Top 80 Sun based Prediction Dates
Jan-14	4, 19, 24 and 27-28	None	6, 8, 14, 19, 21-28, 31	11, 15, 24-25, 29-31
Feb-14	6, 18-19 and 24	None	2-5, 7, 9, 17-28	1, 5, 7-9, 11, 13-14, 17-19, 21-22, 25, 27
Mar-14	1, 3-5, 8-10, 12-17, 19-28, 30-31	None	1-2, 9-13, 20-21, 24-25	2, 6, 11, 13, 18, 20, 23, 27, 30
Apr-14	1-3, 7-13, 15, 17-18, 20-21, 26-27, 30	1(8.2), 3(7.7), 11(7.1), 12(7.6), 13(7.4), 18(7.2), 19(7.5)	3, 17	2, 6, 18, 21
May-14	1, 5, 7-8, 10-15, 17-18, 24, 26, 31	None	None	1, 7, 8, 10, 29
Jun-14	6-7, 19, 21, 23, 25-26	23(7.9)	22-23, 27-29	17, 23-24, 26-27
Jul-14	1, 8, 10, 13-20, 22-23, 25, 28	None	2, 7-8, 13-14, 16-18, 20, 22-25, 27-28	11-12, 24, 30
Aug-14	2, 12, 24-25, 27-28	None	4-5	1, 6, 21, 27

Sep-14	1-2, 6, 12, 15, 20, 22, 24, 26-27	None	16, 19, 30
Oct-14	8-9, 11-12, *14*-15, 17, 19, 20-23, 27-28, 30-31	9(7), 14(7.3)	12-13, 17-18, 20	1-3, 6, 8-*9*, 11-12, *14*, 16, 18, 26-28, 30
Nov-14	*1-2*, 5-8, 10, 12, 15-17, 23-24, 26	1(7.1), 15(7.1)	4-7, 9, 11, *15*, 17-19, 21-26, 28, 30	*1-2*, 5-6, 9-10, *15*-17, 19-21, 28-30
Dec-14	3-7, 9-11, 16, 18, 25, 28-29	None	1-4, 6-11, 14, 16-21, 24-27	1, 5, 9-11, 26, 28, 30

no-Moon top 16 all-planet based model predicts one of them while the 626-variable no-Moon top 80 sun based model accurately predicts both of them. Please note that these models pick 18 and 15 days respectively in November 2014 for the earthquake of magnitude 7 or higher. The previous geocentric longitude based model III picked 14 days for that month and predicted both earthquakes accurately.

Earthquake Predictions for 2011-2014 of Magnitude 7 or Higher

Table 4 lists the prediction dates for Model III and two types (576 variable top 16 all-planet and 626 variable top 80 sun based) of Model IV and the actual dates on which the earthquakes of magnitude 7 or higher occurred for the period starting from January 2011 through December 2014. The first two columns in Table 2 list months and the prediction dates for Model III for the corresponding months. The next column lists the dates on which earthquakes occurred with magnitude shown in the parentheses. If the prediction date matches the actual date, the prediction date is highlighted in italics in the prediction column. The last two columns in Table 4 list the prediction dates for two types of Model IV. Again, if the prediction date matches the actual date, the prediction date in these columns is highlighted in italics.

As shown in Table 4, the overall monthly predicted dates ranged between 0 to 24 days for both Model III and Model IV with monthly average predicted dates were about the same for both Model III and Model IV. In other words the model rules out, on monthly average basis, between 16 to 22 days.

Model III

Table 5 summarizes the results for the earthquakes of magnitude 7 or higher for Model III. The first two columns in Table-4, the years and the corresponding number of predicted dates are listed. In the next two columns the number of suc-

Table-5

Model III

(Two sets: with and without Moon Models with two cases each)

Year and Model	P days	No. of Hits	Actual No. of EQs	P days/Total	Probability Bionomial
880 Var Model					
2011	108	11	17	0.29589	0.002866
2012	38	3	15	0.103825	0.198989
2013	84	3	17	0.230137	0.786237
2014	98	4	12	0.268493	0.40901
Overall	328	21	61	0.224658	0.022156
410 Var Model					
2011	116	6	17	0.317808	0.467002
2012	96	4	15	0.262295	0.582224
2013	104	7	17	0.284932	0.184442
2014	124	8	12	0.339726	0.021157
Overall	440	25	61	0.30137	0.046638
720 Var wo Mn Model					
2011	71	9	17	0.194521	0.002107
2012	53	3	15	0.144809	0.373061
2013	116	4	17	0.317808	0.839101
2014	104	8	12	0.284932	0.006746
Overall	344	24	61	0.235616	0.004347
280 Var wo Mn Model					
2011	83	4	17	0.227397	0.562633
2012	104	3	15	0.284153	0.84392
2013	104	7	17	0.284932	0.184442
2014	96	3	12	0.263014	0.648549

cessful predicted earthquakes and the number of earthquakes occurred are shown. The fifth column shows the ratio of predicted days with the total number of days for that year. The last column lists the calculated probability. The probability calculations are based on the binomial distribution probability and are calculated using the Microsoft Excel statistical func-

Table-6
Model III (Combined 410 and 720 variable models)

Year	P days	No. of Hits	Actual No. of EQs	P days/Total	Probability Bionomial
2011	135	13	17	0.369863	0.001081
2012	115	6	15	0.314208	0.321263
2013	154	8	17	0.421918	0.431439
2014	162	11	12	0.443836	0.000937
Overall	566	38	61	0.387671	0.00017

tion BINOM.DIST, according to this function the probability is calculated as:

Calculated probability = 1-BINOMDIST (# of hits-1, actual # of EQs, predicted days/365, TRUE)

Thus, for year 2011 there were 17 earthquakes of magnitude 7 or higher and the 720 variable without-Moon model, by picking 71 days out of 365, correctly predicted 9 earthquakes. The probability of that prediction according binomial probability distribution is 0.2 percent. In other words, there is only 0.2 percent chance to correctly predict 9 out of 17 earthquakes by picking 71 days out of 365.

For each of the four models (or cases), the overall probability of prediction for the four years (2011-2014) is also shown at the bottom of each model. It ranged from 0.4 percent (0.004) to 45 percent (0.45), with the best performance by the 720 variable model no-Moon Model. Note that as the probability number decreases the model performance improves.

Further, the Model III was improved by combining 410 variable with-Moon model case with the 720 variable without-Moon model case. The results of the combined model are shown in Table 6. The overall probability of the combined model for the four year period is 0.017 percent as opposed to the best performing 720 variable without-Moon model with

0.4347 percent overall probability. This improvement is due to the fact that there was a great deal of overlap for the prediction dates and the only 11 out of 38 earthquakes were predicted by the both model cases.

Table 7 summarizes the results for the earthquakes of magnitude 7 or higher for Top 16 most frequently occurred declination angles of Model IV. The first two columns in Table 7, the years and the corresponding number of predicted dates are listed. In the next two columns the number of successful predicted earthquakes and the number of earthquakes occurred are shown. The fifth column shows the ratio of predicted days with the total number of days for that year. The last column lists the calculated binomial probability. Thus, for year 2011 there were 17 earthquakes of magnitude 7 or higher, and the 576 variable without-Moon model, by picking 110 days out of 365, correctly predicted 8 earthquakes. The probability of that prediction according binomial probability distribution is 10.7 percent. In other words, there is only a 10.7 percent chance to correctly predict 8 out of 17 earthquakes by picking 110 days out of 365days.

For each of the four models (cases), the overall probability of prediction for the four years (2011-2014) is also shown at the bottom of each model case. It ranged from 23.7 percent (0.2367) to 77 percent (0.777), with the best performance by the 576 variable case (23.7 percent) no-Moon Model. Note that as the probability number decreases the model performance improves.

Model IV (Top 80 Most Frequently Occurring Sun Based Declination Angles)

Table 8 summarizes the results for the earthquakes of magnitude 7 or higher for Top 80 most frequently occurred, sun based declination angles of Model IV. The first two columns in Table 8, the years and the corresponding number of pre-

Table-7
(Two sets: with and without Moon Models with two cases each)

Year and Model	P days	No. of Hits	Actual No. of EQs	P days/Total	Probability Bionomial
720 Var Model					
2011	122	6	17	0.334247	0.525559
2012	48	2	15	0.131148	0.603758
2013	98	6	17	0.268493	0.293885
2014	111	1	12	0.30411	0.987103
Overall	379	15	61	0.259589	0.643996
308 Var Model					
2011	114	5	17	0.312329	0.653017
2012	58	1	15	0.15847	0.92483
2013	103	6	17	0.282192	0.340441
2014	111	2	12	0.30411	0.91947
Overall	386	14	61	0.264384	0.774203
576 Var wo Mn Model					
2011	110	8	17	0.30137	0.107008
2012	42	2	15	0.114754	0.52689
2013	99	5	17	0.271233	0.506897
2014	111	3	12	0.30411	0.75691
Overall	362	18	61	0.247945	0.236792
244 Var wo Mn Model					
2011	164	7	17	0.449315	0.7078
2012	84	2	15	0.229508	0.890515
2013	155	7	17	0.424658	0.633086
2014	133	4	12	0.364384	0.691173
Overall	536	20	61	0.367123	0.777431

dicted dates are listed. In the next two columns the number of successful predicted earthquakes and the number of earthquakes occurred are shown. The fifth column shows the ratio of predicted days with the total number of days for that year. The last column lists the calculated binomial probability. Thus, for year 2014 there were 12 earthquakes of magnitude 7 or higher, and the 626 variable without-Moon model, by picking 94 days out of 365, correctly predicted 6 earthquakes. The

Table-8
(Sun based -Two sets: with and without Moon Models with two cases each)

Year and Model	P days	No. of Hits	Actual No. of EQs	P days/Total	Probability Bionomial
706 Var Model					
2011	86	5	17	0.23561644	0.371213
2012	61	2	15	0.16666667	0.740378
2013	85	5	17	0.23287671	0.360838
2014	75	3	12	0.20547945	0.460997
Overall	307	15	61	0.21027397	0.292076
344 Var Model					
2011	119	6	17	0.3260274	0.496399
2012	96	6	15	0.26229508	0.176748
2013	120	5	17	0.32876712	0.704977
2014	105	4	12	0.28767123	0.469201
Overall	440	21	61	0.30136986	0.273527
626 Var wo Mn Model					
2011	62	4	17	0.16986301	0.324495
2012	80	3	15	0.21857923	0.668299
2013	132	8	17	0.36164384	0.24399
2014	94	6	12	0.25753425	0.061994
Overall	368	21	61	0.25205479	0.068667
279 Var wo Mn Model					
2011	67	2	17	0.18356164	0.84656
2012	69	3	15	0.18852459	0.55773
2013	63	0	17	0.17260274	#NUM!
2014	137	7	12	0.37534247	0.118266
Overall	336	12	61	0.23013699	0.77655

probability of that prediction according binomial probability distribution is 6.2 percent. In other words, there is only a 6.2 percent chance to correctly predict 8 out of 17 earthquakes by picking 94 days out of 365days.

For each of the four models (cases), the overall probability of prediction for the four years (2011-2014) is also shown at the bottom of each model case. It ranged from 6.2 percent (0.062) to 77.7 percent (0.776), with the best performance by the 626 variable case (6.2 percent) no-Moon Model.

Table-9
(Result Summary)

	P days	No. of Hits	Actual No. of EQs	P days/Total	Probability Bionomial
Model III					
Combined 410 and 720 Var					
2011	135	13	17	0.369863014	0.001081403
2012	115	6	15	0.31420765	0.321262502
2013	154	8	17	0.421917808	0.431439292
2014	162	11	12	0.443835616	0.000937109
Overall	566	38	61	0.387671233	0.000170104
Model IV					
All planet top 16 - 576 Var case					
2011	110	8	17	0.301369863	0.107008142
2012	42	2	15	0.114754098	0.526889881
2013	99	5	17	0.271232877	0.506896736
2014	111	3	12	0.304109589	0.756910006
Overall	362	18	61	0.247945205	0.236792127
Model IV					
Sun based top 80 - 626 var case					
2011	62	4	17	0.169863014	0.324495448
2012	80	3	15	0.218579235	0.668298685
2013	132	8	17	0.361643836	0.24399028
2014	94	6	12	0.257534247	0.061993861
Overall	368	21	61	0.252054795	0.06866742

Conclusions

Table 9 summarizes the results for the Model III and two types of Model IV by choosing the best performing model case in each case.

From the results of probability calculations as listed in Table 9, it can be noted that by minimizing the number of prediction days for the same amount of hits (correctly predicted earthquakes) the model performance improves. Alternately for the same amount of prediction dates the model performance improves if the number of hits increases.

It is interesting to note that all the best performing model cases of Model III and Model IV include the without-Moon model cases. The 720 variable without-Moon case in combination with 410 variable with-Moon case for Model III; and 576 variable without-Moon case for top 16 all planet Model IV and 626 variable without-Moon case for sun based Model IV belong to only without-Moon model cases. As indicated earlier in this paper, the fact that Moon's average daily variation is about 2 declination degrees it can form almost equal number of angles with every other planet during a daily twenty-four hour period thereby nullifying influence of Moon is reflected in these model cases.

Compared to the Model III performance, where the combined 410 with-Moon model case with 720 variable without-Moon model case has the probability of 0.017 percent, the best case of top 16 frequently occurred 576 variable without-Moon case of Model IV performed three orders of magnitude poorly with 23.7 percent probability and the best case of top 80 sun based 626 variable without-Moon case of Model IV performed about two order of magnitudes poorly with 6.8 percent probability.

Clearly, the top 16 frequently occurred 576 variable declination angle Model IV with 23.7 percent probability is not significant in correlating the earthquakes of magnitude seven and higher with the declination angles of all planetary pairs. The sun based top 80 frequently occurred declination angle model IV with 6.8 percent probability is at least one order of magnitude better than the random chance (100% probability). In other words, compared to Model III, the Model IV performance is mediocre; and between the two best cases of Model IV, the sun based 626 variable model IV is better than the top 16 frequently occurred 576 variable model.

It is important to recognize that the model performance varies from one year to the next. The performance of Model III is significantly enhanced for 2014 by correctly predicting 11 out of 12 earthquakes by picking 162 days out of 365 for that year.

The model performance for both Model III and Model IV may need to be observed over a long period of time to confirm the consistency of their performance. Nonetheless, the Model III consistently performed better over all the Model IV cases for 2011-2014.

For the model to be applied for earthquakes of magnitude 7 and higher to predict over a narrower range of days would require further improvement and therefore, more research work is warranted. In addition, further research is necessary regarding the locations of earthquakes.

Acknowledgements

The author wishes to acknowledge the grant provided by Catharine and Ernest Grant Trust for this research work. In addition, the author wants to acknowledge the U.S. Geological Survey Web site for availability of downloading the earthquake data..

References

1. Earthquake Prediction Model presented at the NCGR (National Council for Geocosmic Research) Research Symposium. National Conference: Baltimore, Maryland, March 2007

2. Earthquake Prediction Model II, NCGR Research Journal, Volume 3, Fall/Winter 2012-2013

3. Earthquake Prediction Model III, NCGR Research Journal, Volume 5, Fall 2015

4. Centennial Earthquake Catalog, Engdahl and Villaseñor, 2002http://earthquake.usgs.gov/research/data/centennial.php

5. www.astroinsight.com

6. http://earthquake.usgs.gov/

Appendix A

Top 16 most frequently occurred declination angles for all 45 planetary angle pairs

		1	2	3	4	5	6	7	8	9	10	11	12	13	14	15	16
1	Pl-Ne	33.6	34	2.8	4.4	8.6	33.8	33.2	34.2	3.2	4.2	5	6.6	35	1.2	3.4	4.6
2	Pl-U	0.4	0.6	38.8	38.6	0.2	0	38.4	2.6	22.2	39	12.6	10.4	14.6	25.2	1.6	4.4
3	Pl-Sa	3.8	36	4.2	4.4	1.2	1.6	44.4	3.2	3.4	35.8	0.2	1.8	7.6	43.4	44.2	1.4
4	Pl-Jup	1	8	1.4	4.2	5.2	6.8	7.6	0.6	5	7.4	7.8	0.4	3.4	1.8	4	4.6
5	Pl-Mr	0.4	1.4	2.2	0.8	2.8	3.6	2.6	0.2	1.2	1.8	3.2	5.4	1	1.6	4	5
6	Pl-Ve	1.2	2.4	3.4	4.2	5.2	1.8	2.6	0.2	0.6	1	2.2	2.8	3.2	6.8	0.4	5.4
7	Pl-Mc	0.2	0.4	1	5.8	0.8	3.6	4.8	10.4	0.6	1.4	2	2.6	3	4.2	6.4	7.6
8	Pl-Sun	0.4	1	1.4	0.8	3	0.2	5.4	1.2	2.2	2.8	2	4	11.6	40.2	0.6	3.6
9	Pl-Mn	2.6	0.2	2.4	9.6	0.8	5.8	3	3.2	3.4	1.4	2	2.8	3.8	4.8	6	6.6
10	Ne-U	1.6	1.4	0.8	45.8	0.2	1	1.2	0.4	0.6	46	45.6	5.8	44.2	26.2	10.2	29.2
11	Ne-Sa	2.6	0.2	2.2	0.8	10.2	0.6	2.8	32.2	39.8	1	6.6	34.4	22.2	23.6	1.6	8.6
12	Ne-Jup	1	1.2	0.8	4.6	7.2	6.6	20.8	2.4	0.6	13.4	0.2	1.4	2.8	3.6	7.6	7.8
13	Ne-Mr	1.4	1.6	3	2.2	3.4	4	8.6	0.6	0.8	2	2.4	0.2	1.8	3.2	5	5.2
14	Ne-Ve	1.8	2.4	3.4	4.4	4.6	0.2	5	15.4	0.4	1	3.2	1.4	2	3	35.6	0.8
15	Ne-Mc	1.8	8	0.2	2	2.4	1.6	2.2	2.8	7.2	31.8	1.2	2.6	3.2	3.4	3.6	7.4
16	Ne-Sun	0.4	1.2	0.2	1	4.4	0.8	1.4	1.6	2.6	3	15.8	0.6	2.4	4.6	6	1.8
17	Ne-Mn	3	2.4	6	1	3.2	5	32.8	0.8	2	2.2	5.8	0.2	0.6	2.6	5.2	6.8
18	Ur-Sa	0.4	31.8	0.2	0.8	0.6	19	1.4	2.4	36	1	29	31.2	39.6	39.8	1.2	3
19	Ur-Jup	0.6	0.2	2.6	0.8	36.8	2.8	16	17.8	0.4	3	17.4	16.6	18.2	46.4	1	17
20	Ur-Mr	0.4	3.2	1.4	19.6	16.4	1	3.8	1.6	3.6	4	0.2	0.6	2.8	5.2	5.4	6.6
21	Ur-Ve	3.2	4.6	7	2.4	3	5.8	9.4	13.4	2.8	7.6	0.2	0.6	0.8	2	2.6	4.2
22	Ur-Mc	2.8	6.6	6.4	1.6	0.4	1	2.2	3	0.2	0.6	4.2	5.6	0.8	1.2	2.6	5.8
23	Ur-Sun	0.2	2	1	1.2	1.8	2.6	3	12.4	0	2.2	2.4	3.2	3.8	1.4	8.2	10.4
24	Ur-Mn	3	0.4	0.6	8	1	2.2	17.6	1.6	1.8	4.6	5	6	10.6	14	2.8	3.2
25	Sa-Jup	0.8	1.4	10.4	1	5.6	23.4	2.4	3.2	8.6	0.4	0.6	3	9.6	6.8	8.8	2.6
26	Sa-Mr	4.2	1.4	2	4.4	7.4	1.2	2.4	5.2	9.4	0.8	4.8	5.8	8.6	1.6	1.8	2.2
27	Sa-Ve	2.8	0.4	4	2.2	2.4	2.6	3.6	3.8	4.2	8.6	0.6	1.4	4.8	5.8	0.2	1.8
28	Sa-Mc	9	2.2	0.8	2.8	4	0.6	1.4	2	2.4	9.4	1.6	2.6	5.8	6.4	11	12.8
29	Sa-Sun	0.8	0.4	0.2	1.4	8.2	2.4	1.8	2	1	0.6	1.2	3.6	3.8	8.6	12.6	2.8
30	Sa-Mn	1.2	4	5.6	1.4	5.2	7.2	21.8	4.2	5.8	29.8	0.4	5.4	6.6	9.6	14	14.8
31	Ju-Mr	1	0.6	1.2	1.6	3.4	1.8	3.2	3.6	1.4	2	10	2.4	5	4.6	6.4	8.4
32	Ju-Ve	2.4	0.6	1.8	0.4	2.2	1	2	1.2	6.4	8.6	15	1.6	3.8	2.8	7.8	4
33	Ju-Mc	1.6	1.4	2	7.6	0.6	3.6	4.4	1.2	2.6	6.2	0.2	5.8	0.4	1	2.2	2.4
34	Ju-Sun	0.6	2.2	0.2	1.4	0.8	2	7.2	0.4	1	1.2	3.8	2.4	2.6	3.6	3	3.2
35	Ju-Mn	4.2	9.4	3	1.4	4.6	6.4	13	3.6	0.2	2	3.8	4.4	5	7	10.6	27.2
36	Mr-Ve	1	3	0.6	1.8	0.8	2.6	4	6.4	0.2	1.6	0.4	3.2	4.6	8.6	10	11
37	Mr-Mc	1.2	0.4	3.2	3.4	1.8	0.8	5.8	3	4.4	4.2	0.2	3.8	5.4	8.6	9	3.6
38	Mr-Sun	0.8	0.2	0.6	1.8	13.8	3.4	3.6	4	4.2	1.2	3.2	4.6	11.6	0.4	1.6	2.4
39	Mr-Mn	4.6	2.2	2.8	3	6	1.2	1.8	9.6	2.4	3.2	4.4	5.4	6.2	7.4	8.8	0.2
40	Ve-Mc	0.4	0.6	3.6	1.6	2	3	1.8	1.2	2.4	2.6	5.2	2.2	0.8	0.2	1	2.8
41	Ve-Su	0.2	0.8	0.4	3.6	0.6	1	1.2	2.6	6.6	1.4	2.8	4.8	1.6	3.2	4.6	4.4
42	Vn-Mn	0.2	1	2.2	4	5.2	4.4	14.8	1.2	1.4	3	6.2	6.8	7.8	18.8	2.8	4.6
43	Mc-Su	1.8	2.6	2.2	1.2	1.4	2.8	2.4	0.8	1.6	3.6	3.4	4.2	0.4	1	5	0.2
44	Mc-Mn	2.8	1.8	3	8.8	3.8	4.4	5.4	13.4	11	18	21	1.4	2.4	5.6	7.4	9.8
45	Su-Mn	2	1.4	3	4.4	5.4	1.2	2.2	2.4	3.8	5.8	7	9.8	2.8	5.2	6	7.6

Appendix B

Top 80 Sun based Declination Angle Numbers for each pair

	Pl-Sun 1	Ne-Sun 2	Ur-Sun 3	Sa-Sun 4	Ju-Sun 5	Mr-Sun 6	Ve-Su 7	Mc-Su 8	Su-Mn 9
1	0.4	0.4	0.2	0.8	0.6	0.8	0.2	1.8	2
2	1	1.2	2	0.4	2.2	0.2	0.8	2.6	1.4
3	1.4	0.2	1	0.2	0.2	0.6	0.4	2.2	3
4	0.8	1	1.2	1.4	1.4	1.8	3.6	1.2	4.4
5	3	4.4	1.8	8.2	0.8	13.8	0.6	1.4	5.4
6	0.2	0.8	2.6	2.4	2	3.4	1	2.8	1.2
7	5.4	1.4	3	1.8	7.2	3.6	1.2	2.4	2.2
8	1.2	1.6	12.4	2	0.4	4	2.6	0.8	2.4
9	2.2	2.6	0	1	1	4.2	6.6	1.6	3.8
10	2.8	3	2.2	0.6	1.2	1.2	1.4	3.6	5.8
11	2	15.8	2.4	1.2	3.8	3.2	2.8	3.4	7
12	4	0.6	3.2	3.6	2.4	4.6	4.8	4.2	9.6
13	11.6	2.4	3.8	3.8	2.6	11.6	1.6	0.4	2.8
14	40.2	4.6	1.4	8.6	3.6	0.4	3.2	1	5.2
15	0.6	6	8.2	12.6	3	1.6	4.6	5	6
16	3.6	1.8	10.4	2.8	3.2	2.4	4.4	0.2	7.6
17	1.6	6.8	1.6	3.2	5.6	2.6	3	4.6	16.6
18	2.6	8.2	4.4	6.2	7.8	6.4	2.2	6.2	20.6
19	6.4	21.8	7.6	2.2	0	5.6	2.4	2	0.4
20	8	30	13.2	2.6	5.8	6.8	3.8	3	0.8
21	6.6	3.2	0.4	3	6.4	9	5.8	7.2	3.2
22	7.2	3.6	0.8	5.2	8.8	11.2	6.2	0.6	3.6
23	7.6	5.6	2.8	17.4	3.4	1.4	8.8	3.2	4.8
24	1.8	14.4	3.6	4.2	4	2.2	4	5.2	10
25	4.4	17.8	4.8	4.6	7.6	2.8	4.2	5.4	12.2
26	4.6	45.4	5.2	5.4	9.6	3.8	5.4	5.8	0.2
27	5.2	2	5.6	5.8	11.2	5	11.2	6	1
28	6.2	2.2	5.8	6.8	11.4	6.6	1.8	6.6	4.6
29	6.8	2.8	6.6	9	11.6	2	8.4	6.8	6.2
30	9.6	3.4	7.2	10	11.8	5.8	0	3.8	6.6
31	12.8	4	7.4	12	12	7.2	6.4	4.4	7.8
32	15.2	4.2	10.8	1.6	13.8	7.4	8	4.8	8
33	42.2	6.6	11.2	5	16	8.6	7.4	7.4	8.2
34	45.8	7.4	13.4	6.6	1.6	13.2	16.6	8.8	8.4
35	5	7.6	14.6	9.4	10.8	3	6	4	10.8
36	7.8	8.8	17.6	12.2	12.8	5.4	10.8	5.6	11.4
37	8.2	12.6	38.4	17	13.4	8	12.6	8.2	12.4
38	16	15	0.6	19.8	15.4	0	17.2	6.4	23.4
39	17	16	4	4.8	17.2	11	5	7.6	35.8
40	19.2	16.2	5	7	19.4	15.8	5.6	7.8	3.4

Appendix B (Continue)

Top 80 Sun based Declination Angle Numbers for each pair

	Pl-Sun 1	Ne-Sun 2	Ur-Sun 3	Sa-Sun 4	Ju-Sun 5	Mr-Sun 6	Ve-Su 7	Mc-Su 8	Su-Mn 9
41	36.8	20.6	6	9.2	22.2	16.2	9	8.4	4
42	37.4	29.4	8	14	4.6	21	9.2	7	5.6
43	38.8	3.8	9.4	15.4	5.2	1	9.4	9	6.4
44	3.4	5.2	9.6	15.6	6	4.4	12.8	12.2	11.6
45	3.8	7.2	11.6	16.6	6.2	4.8	7	0	12.8
46	4.8	9.8	18.8	18.2	8	5.2	9.8	8	13.8
47	5.6	11.4	19	22.6	10.6	6	10.2	8.6	14.2
48	5.8	14.6	24.4	22.8	13.2	7	12	9.6	15.2
49	7	14.8	26.2	30.6	15.2	8.8	2	9.8	15.8
50	10.4	18.2	4.6	36.6	16.6	10.4	6.8	10.2	17.6
51	11.4	19.4	5.4	3.4	16.8	10.8	7.6	12.4	18.6
52	11.8	23.6	6.2	4	19	11.4	8.2	9.2	19.4
53	21.2	25.2	6.4	7.2	31	11.8	10.4	9.4	24.4
54	26.8	32.8	7	7.4	32.4	15.2	10.6	10	4.2
55	34	37	11.4	8	1.8	15.4	11.8	11.2	6.8
56	34.6	39.6	12.2	8.8	4.2	15.6	14.4	11.8	9.2
57	42.6	5.8	12.6	11	5	16	15	12.6	11.8
58	2.4	7.8	13.6	11.2	5.4	20.4	16.8	11.6	15.4
59	4.2	8.4	14.4	11.4	6.6	7.6	7.8	10.4	15.6
60	7.4	11.2	14.8	11.8	8.2	12.4	10	10.6	17.8
61	8.8	13.6	17.2	13.6	8.4	18.4	11	10.8	18.4
62	9.2	16.8	21.2	14.2	9.8	22.6	11.4	12.8	19.6
63	12.2	17.4	22.6	14.8	10.4	27.4	11.6	12	20
64	14	19	24	16.2	12.2	9.8	14	13.2	21.4
65	14.2	21.6	25.6	16.8	15	14	14.8	11.4	23.8
66	19.4	23	34.6	17.2	17.4	14.2	15.4	13	25
67	21.8	36.6	40.4	18.8	18	15	15.8	11	34.4
68	24.2	38	43.6	21.6	19.8	19.6	17		37.6
69	24.4	38.8	4.2	24.2	20.4	19.8	3.4		38.2
70	24.8	4.8	6.8	24.6	22.6	25.4	5.2		38.4
71	25.8	6.2	7.8	31.4	23.6	7.8	7.2		39.8
72	27.6	6.4	8.4	32.6	25.6	8.4	9.6		41.8
73	30.2	9	9.2	39	28.2	9.2	13		0.6
74	30.4	9.2	10.2	5.6	29.4	9.6	13.2		2.6
75	33.4	10.2	13.8	12.4	29.6	10.6	13.8		9.8
76	33.6	10.6	16.2	13	30.4	12.2	16		11.2
77	35.2	11	17	13.8	33.8	16.8	13.6		12.6
78	36	11.6	17.4	15.8	2.8	17.4	16.2		13.2
79	37	13.8	18	18.4	4.4	17.6	12.4		13.4
80	38.2	14	19.6	19.2	4.8	19	16.4		14

Sun Square Neptune

Narcissism vs. Quietism:
Can We Change the Narrative?

By Branimira Maldeghem

ABSTRACT: This research explores the archetypal relationship between Sun and Neptune, the underlying psychological dynamics as reflected in the square aspect between them, the psychological defences employed in resolving the conflict [of the square], and the multiplicity of outcomes consistent with the level of integration of the aspect. My hypothesis is that the expression of the psychological dynamics of the square between Sun and Neptune operates on a continuum between narcissism and quietism. Narcissism, in brief, can be defined as ego-inflation and quietism as self-transcendence. The potential resolution of the psychological conflict inherent in this aspect lies in awareness that the negation of free will is rooted in self-defeating beliefs. The integrated expression of the aspect would entail deeper understanding of how individual intentionality can operate within the collective will. It would involve a conscious choice to redefine oneself by finding a "modus operandi" between personal will and whatever transcends it—be it a visionary societal ideal or a higher spiritual power. Through fantasy and imagination, artistic works provide a safe outlet for reenactment of traumatic past experiences in the hope of finding a different, more positive and self-affirming resolution thereof. My hypothesis will be tested by an interpretation of the psychological dynamics of Sun square Neptune as reflected in the life experiences and artistic works of the French filmmaker Jean-Luc Godard.

Theoretical Framework

My astrological interpretation will be based on the theoretical paradigm of AstroPsychology[1], as developed by Glenn Perry, PhD.

> The horoscope is interpreted as an ever-evolving personal narrative around core psychological conflicts as reflected in the birth chart. Perry asserts: *"Because every chart tells a story, we can utilize a narrative metaphor in explaining the principle of chart interpretation. Planets symbolise the story's characters; signs represent their underlying motives; houses depict the various settings that provide a background for the story's action; aspects signify the quality of relationships between characters; and dispositors and significators reveal the overall plot or story line of the chart. ...[the] plot involves a pattern that ideally constitutes a path of evolutionary unfoldment...modifies awareness and leads toward a progressive development and integration of character."*[i] ... '*Perhaps the horoscope is best understood as symbolizing an unfolding story in which fate is altered by the development and unfoldment of the character.*'[ii]

In AstroPsychology, planetary characters are unique, complex, multi-dimensional beings. They operate within "fixed rules" (chart variables) but employ "flexible strategies" (free choices) in order to re-write their stories and re-define themselves.

Research Methodology

My research employs a hermeneutic method as applied to content analysis and an in-depth study of biographies, artistic works, and interviews pertinent to the personal and artistic journey of Jean-Luc Godard.

My narrative approach to natal chart interpretation applies Perry's developmental age method (DAM). The main premise of the DAM is that astrological archetypes also signify developmental stages of fixed duration within the human life cycle.

> Perry suggests: *"Each sign can be understood as a developmental stage of specific quality and duration. And because houses are based on the same angular dynamics as the signs to which they correspond, they also represent the same 12 stage process. While the zodiac shows the genetic unfolding of consciousness, the houses reveal the native's actual experience during particular periods. This occurs by virtue of planets signaling not only where but when that planetary process will be most acute."*[iii]

A planet's house position specifies the exact year and month during which the meaning of that configuration is acutely felt or expressed[2]. Furthermore, there is a diachronistic relationship between planets in aspect with each other. This can be understood as a meaningful relationship between events from different stages that are expressions of the same planetary aspect. Earlier events are analogous to and preparatory for experiences occurring during the stage symbolized by the later planet. In the case of Godard, my analysis will focus on the planetary age of his Sun (5.4) and Neptune (72.6). Consideration will also be given to Jupiter (56.2) as dispositor of the Sun and Mars (64.4) as disposed by the Sun.

Developmental Age Ranges by Sign/House[iv]

Sign/House	Age Range
Aries/1st house	0-2
Taurus/2nd house	2-5
Gemini/3rd house	5-9
Cancer/4th house	9-14
Leo/5th house	14-20
Virgo/6th house	20-27
Libra/7th house	27-35
Scorpio/8th house	35-44
Sagittarius/9th house	44-54
Capricorn/10th house	54-65
Aquarius/11th house	65-77
Pisces/12th house	77-90

Calculated Planetary Ages for Godard

Planet	Planetary age	Relevant years
Sun	5.4	March, 1936 (1935-1937)
Jupiter	56.2	January, 1987 (1986-1988)
Mars	64.4	March, 1995 (1994-1996)
Neptune	72.6	May, 2003 (2002-2004)

The orbs used for the interpretation of the aspects between planets are as follows:

Aspect	Applying orb	Separating orb
Conjunction	10	8
Opposition	9	7
Trine	8	7
Square	7	6
Sextile	4	3
Quincunx	4	3

Purpose of the Research

The purpose of this research is to deepen understanding of the archetypal conflict inherent in the Sun-Neptune square by exploring its concrete manifestations. My conclusions will hopefully enrich astrology by providing an evidence-based, more nuanced understanding of the multiplicity of outcomes reflective of the aspect at different levels of integration. They could further reinforce the utility of qualitative research in natal chart interpretation, as its application can expand, interconnect, and transform our understanding of astrological phenomena.

While this research is intended to be sound—that is, coherent and comprehensive—it is also subject to certain limitations linked to the fact that in the process of co-creating meaning, my interpretations are influenced to a certain extent by personal values and biases. Therefore, I will refrain from claiming absolute validity of my conclusions. They are intended to be well substantiated, evidence-based probability judgments.

Archetypal Dynamics of Sun Square Neptune

Archetypes are universal organizing principles inherent in nature. They are an animating and formative pattern of energy that connects individual souls to the cosmic soul[v].

For the purpose of this research, astrological archetypes are interpreted as 12 phases of a 360-degree cycle, thus angles, associated with different principles of life and having different meanings: beginnings (Aries), creativity (Leo), endings (Pisces), and so forth.[vi] Each phase (sign) derives its meaning from its angular relationship with the beginning of the cycle, zero degrees Aries. Different astrological variables of sign, house, and aspect are all features of a single astrological archetype, as they share a kinship of meaning due to their correspondence to the same angle. A planet is the archetype in its action mode, a sign is its motivational mode, a house is its contextual mode, and an aspect is its relational mode. For example, the first 120 degrees from Aries is the phase relationship of Leo, fifth house, and the opening trine, all of which share similar meanings as variations of the opening 120-degree angle.

Astrological archetypes are corollary to both process (subjective psychological phenomena) and content (objective environmental phenomena).They are multidimensional in that each astrological variable can symbolize a psychological function, a state of mind or attitude, and a behavioural trait, and at the same time an external character, place, thing, or event. They are polyvalent as they combine with other variables (signs, houses, and aspects), which modify their expression in various ways. They operate on a continuum of integration ranging from less to more functional expressions and are indeterminate in concrete outcome since their manifestation evolves over time[vii].

The Sun: Evolution of Personal Identity from Ego to Self

The Sun is associated with our creative self-expression. It is our core that wants to shine and illuminate, to be seen and recognized for who one really is, to be acclaimed for one's creations and applauded for one's performance.

As a psychological faculty, it represents our Ego/Self. Our ego is the capacity to will, identify, and create, which establishes boundaries that differentiate self from environment. We consciously identify with what falls within our ego boundaries and remain unconscious as to what remains beyond. By shifting these boundaries in accord with conscious self-awareness, we construct our personal identity or self-concept.

Whoever we decide we are, we need to be recognized as special and unique by the "audience" of our social environment. For this to happen, our ego "as the conscious, self-aware portion of the personality"[viii] defends identity from being overwhelmed by the collective dimensions of the psyche. Our journey of "becoming" needs to feel safe. Therefore, our ego suppresses and keeps out of awareness threatening thoughts, feelings, and impulses.

The organized system of ideas constituting our personal identity or self-concept is to some extent an arbitrary construct, a personal myth, attributing to us a certain role, and demanding that we wear a given mask. Perry defines it as "a strategy designed to assure approval and avoid disapproval" developed through relationships with significant others (parents), being a "necessary trance" for the first half of life and dominating one's consciousness, once established, unless challenged[ix].

Constructed self-images replace the true leader of the personality—the Self—which Jung defined as an expression of psychic wholeness that transcends but includes the ego.[x] The Self is "the center and the circumference of the psyche," which includes both conscious and unconscious content, while the ego-self system functions as an organized pride system protecting the person from defeat and embarrassment.

For the Sun to become a true leader of the personality; that is, an actualized "Self," the ego must constantly evolve by identifying with, balancing, and integrating all its psychological drives. Astrologically, this is reflected in "integrating the polarized sign-pairs of the zodiac and their respective ruling planets into unified whole"[xi]. The process of dissolving the polarity of, for example, independence versus engagement (Aries-Libra) into a unique blend of independence "and" engagement creates new, higher-level abilities. It elevates us to the status of conscious creators of our personal narratives.

Neptune: Transcending the Self in Pursuit of Unity

Neptune is associated with the ideal for transcendence and infinite love and beauty. It signifies the part of us that longs to belong to an all-inclusive whole wherein personal identity does not matter and all divisions and conflict is reconciled.

Neptune reflects our imagination, our capacity for dreams, fantasy and idealism. It inspires us with visions and spiritual ideals of how to reach this state of "unity" with life and God. However, these ideals turn into mere illusions when we try to transcend existing differences by simply denying them. The resulting utopian state where "fantasy [is substituted] for reality. . . by superimposing the ideal over the real"[xii] can lead to disillusionment, leaving us deceived, filled with guilt, and victimized.

The malleability of Neptune poses risks of deception, but it also offers the gift of psychic attunement to the collective unconscious, the compass of our intuition that we could let navigate us.

Neptune has the overwhelming power to dissolve and loosen the boundaries we build around us. When unable to tolerate this "threat," we feel confused and helpless. We either collapse into chaos or try to defend against it by denying, escaping, and retreating to a safe imaginary place. We tend to procrastinate and abdicate responsibility. We become submissive and defer to others. We put on a mask to disguise ourselves in hopes of becoming "unseen." In other words, we self-sabotage and undo ourselves.

When, on the contrary, we are ready to follow the Neptunian calling to accept our sometimes painful reality, we must utilize our capacity for empathy, compassion, and forgiveness. Such capacities allow us to relieve our suffering and learn lessons of sacrifice, humility, and dependence on a higher power.

Neptune whispers to us that we can aspire to be someone else. It infuses us with inspiration to go beyond our constructed selves. It offers us the gift of having an inspired existence, experiencing the divine by "letting go and letting God."

Dynamics of the (Opening) Square: The Need to Belong and the Fear of Rejection

Planetary aspects reflect the way planets communicate with, penetrate and transfuse each other. Aspects may operate as cognitions ("personal myths") that underlay our internal talk and synchronistically construct the world of outer experience. In this sense, aspects reflect our ability to bridge our self- and world-concepts and provide us with sense of identity and life purpose.

The square is considered to be a hard, yin aspect of inhibition and restraint. Archetypally, it entails a conflict between conscious (yang) and unconscious (yin). Perry[xiii] argues that the psychodynamics of the square implies reciprocal influence and mutual resistance between the involved planets. They operate at cross-purposes and challenge each other's values and right of expression. Usually, the slower-moving planet tends to impose its agenda on the faster-moving one. The latter, feeling inhibited, would attempt to resist the pressure and to defend itself while struggling to accommodate the necessary demands of the slower moving planet. The dynamics of the square can be subjectively experienced as a state of doubt, fear, and frustration in relation to the planetary functions involved. It could transpire in self- and world-concepts based on an unconscious grim belief, operating as an intra-psychic blockage that may manifest externally as situations of impasse.

Psychological defenses employed to cope with anxieties inherent in the square are: repression, projection, devaluation, acting out, and passive aggression. They create a psychic imbalance due to the hypertrophication (overdevelopment) of the planetary function that is consciously expressed (overcompensation) and the hypofunctioning of the other that is repressed and projected ("shadow" creation).

Here I would like to elaborate on the quality and meaning of the *opening* square. According to Perry,[xiv] an aspect derives its meaning from the nature of the sign that constitutes the angle in the natural zodiac. An opening square corresponds to the first 90 degrees in the natural zodiac and therefore bears a Cancerian meaning. Accordingly, any square occurring when a faster planet forms the first 90 degree angle with a slower planet during their synodic cycle (as in the case of Godard's Sun square Neptune), is defined as an "opening" square. It would therefore exhibit Cancerian meanings and qualities, pose Cancerian challenges and require Canrcerian solutions.

The opening square may engender fear that if the planetary functions are expressed wrongly, we will be unloved and rejected. When the two planetary functions are not appropriately contained, we could be dominated by emotions, become reactive, and inappropriately display anger and insensitivity. We could experience periodic upheavals that cause distress, subsequent rejection, and hurt feelings.[xv]

At the same time, the opening square functions in the manner of "initiation cuts."[xvi] Through experiences involving the planets forming the opening square, we are initiated into the world of feelings. There we may feel tender, protective, and caring. Integration of this aspect requires constant review of our course of action, reflection on our personal history, containment of the two conflicting planetary functions, and integration of the repressed psychic material.

Integration of Sun (Opening) Square Neptune: Multiplicity of Outcomes

The Sun-Leo drive for validation and appreciation is reflected in the principles of intentionality, identification, and creativity. The Neptune-Pisces drive for transcendence is reflected in the principles of spiritual unity, sacrifice, and redemption.

The Sun wills so that we can be "rulers" of our destiny, constructs our identity so that we can become authentic "heroes," creates to actualize our divine, God-given talents. Neptune strives for all-inclusive, indiscriminate "oneness" with life and God by blurring boundaries, dissolving, and renunciating attachments.

Whereas the Sun is concerned with free will and attachment to preferred outcomes, Neptune reminds us that these are just illusions and that nothing is permanent. Whereas the Sun believes that control over our decisions is all that matters, Neptune evokes feelings of surrender and trust in a higher power. Whereas the Sun requires us to differentiate and distinguish ourselves, Neptune whispers that we must go beyond individual needs and identity in order to transcend individual selfhood and partake in collective consciousness.

The square involves a conflict between the different agendas of Sun and Neptune: between ego (separateness) and Higher Self (transcendent wholeness), between self-will (attachment) and God's will (letting go and letting God), and between validation (ego/pride) and forgiveness (atonement/salvation). This intrapsychic conflict is rooted in the perception that the involved planetary functions are mutually exclusive. In the case of the *opening* square, the conflict can be premised as: "Will I be lovable (square) if I wish to be special (Sun) at the expense of the collective or contrary to the Divine will (Neptune)? Will I be rejected (square) if I identify solely with my immediate ego interests (Sun) instead of acting on behalf of a larger whole (Neptune)? Will I be accepted (square) if my free will (Sun) disregards the interest of the collective or leads to someone else's suffering (Neptune)?"

The resolution of the conflict and thus the integration of the aspect require differentiation and integration of both archetypes and their balancing within the psyche. Perry asserts that aspects are expressed on a continuum from disintegrated to integrated states. This continuum can be conceptualized in terms of five levels: neurotic, low functioning, conventional, high-functioning, and self-actualized.[xvii] Individuals evolve over time along this continuum wherein each higher level transcends but includes the lower, adds new possibilities of expression, more freedom, a broader range of behavior and experience, increased functionality, and greater satisfaction.

Based on this premise, my hypothesis is that expression of the Sun-Neptune square operates on a continuum between narcissism (neurotic) and quietism (self-transcendence).

When the Neptunian imperative threatens the solar "target state" of pride and confidence, the native may experience over-modulated solar states of deflation and low self-esteem. He may feel invisible and discounted, confused and disillusioned, paralyzed and unable to take a stance, and wracked by irrational guilt. All of this may culminate in acts of self-undoing.

To defend against Neptunian collapse into nothingness, the native may split the solar archetype into "all good" (internalized) and "all bad" (repressed and projected) qualities. Resultant pathogenic bi-polar beliefs range from self-aggrandizement (overvaluation) to self-abnegation (devaluation) and can manifest as an unstable sense of self.

If the person feels worthless inside, he may overcompensate by appropriating Neptunian idealism for solar purposes. He may construct a compensatory "fantasy" self that displays under-modulated solar states of hubris and grandiosity—in other words, *narcissism*.

For the purposes of this research, narcissism is understood as a continuum of egocentric traits at different levels of intensity.[3] Narcissistic traits may produce a grandiose sense of self-importance, fantasies of boundless success, a sense of being special and unique, a need for excessive admiration, an exaggerated sense of entitlement, arrogance, lack of empathy for others, feelings of superiority, omnipotence, envy and contempt, and a tendency to be interpersonally exploitive. When Neptune predominates, the individual may manifest *inverted narcissism.* Holding back to avoid envy, he unconsciously assumes responsibility for the suffering of others, attracts experiences of tragedy and loss, and becomes the victim of people exhibiting narcissistic traits. He may appear to be shy, but is nonetheless secretly grandiose.

On the other side of the continuum is the alternative strategy of *quietism*: self-transcendence by renunciation of self-will coupled with devotion to a spiritual ideal. In its broadest sense, quietism refers to any spiritual practice that seeks to negate human will in order to achieve ecstatic enlightenment[xviii]. It implies intentional self-annihilation and absorption of soul into the Divine for the sake of spiritual growth and unity with the Divine.[xix] Quietism reflects the ultimate Neptunian ideal of spiritual union through "letting go and letting God." It demands to bring *"the soul to a true annihilation of itself [that] must be in a man's own judgment, in his will. [The] happy soul…, because God lives [therein], is changed, spiritualized, transformed, and deified".*[xx]

On the continuum between narcissism and quietism, our answer to the question on how to adjust the individual will (Sun) to the interests of a larger all-inclusive whole (Neptune) can lead to a multiplicity of outcomes contingent upon level of integration of the aspect. These answers, for example, might demonstrate whether one suffers writer's block or has a burst of inspiration to rewrite the Sun-Neptune chapter of his or her life story.

At lower levels of integration, the individual craves inspiration: he may be deceived, dispossessed, and abandoned, a hopeless victim; he could be imprisoned, addicted, and enslaved. At higher levels of integration, he inspires self-transcendence through selfless service to humanity for the sake of an ideal: He is a political visionary, savior, or martyr interested in the cause and relief of suffering. He may channel divine wisdom by exhibiting boundless faith, dream the ideal and pursue the dream, in which case he is a mystic philosopher, spiritual leader, depth psychologist, or astrologer. He may also be a divinely inspired artist who gives creative expression to Neptunian themes through imagistic art forms such as painting, photography, poetry, music, dance, and cinema.

Jean-Luc Godard: The Filmmaker as Philosopher

"We walk through ourselves, meeting robbers, ghosts, giants, old men, young men, wives, widows, brothers in law. But always meeting ourselves."—J. Joyce

Jean-Luc Godard is a Franco-Swiss filmmaker and a leading member of the "French New Wave."[4] Known for stylistic innovations that challenged the conventions of Hollywood cinema, he is universally recognized as the most audacious, radical, and influential of the "New Wave" filmmakers. His work reflects a fervent knowledge of film history, a comprehensive understanding of existential and Marxist philosophy, and profound insight into the fragility of human relations. His career has been devoted to both honoring and destroying cinema, taking it apart and rebuilding it. Godard represents the filmmaker as philosopher, "the number theorist"[xxi] who "conjugates" the prime numbers of social reality to create a comprehensible pattern.

His movies explore the nature of time and consciousness, the problem of language and communication, and the questions of causality and human freedom. To a small coterie of cinephiles and most professional film critics, especially in Europe, Godard is considered the ultimate cinematic genius. To others, his films often seem insufferably opaque and indecipherable. His works have been a source of inspiration for many directors, including Martin Scorsese, Quentin Tarantino, Woody Allen, Steven Soderbergh, Jim Jarmusch, and Wong Kar-wai.

The Sun in Godard's chart is in Sagittarius in the third house. Sagittarius is associated with the search for meaning and need

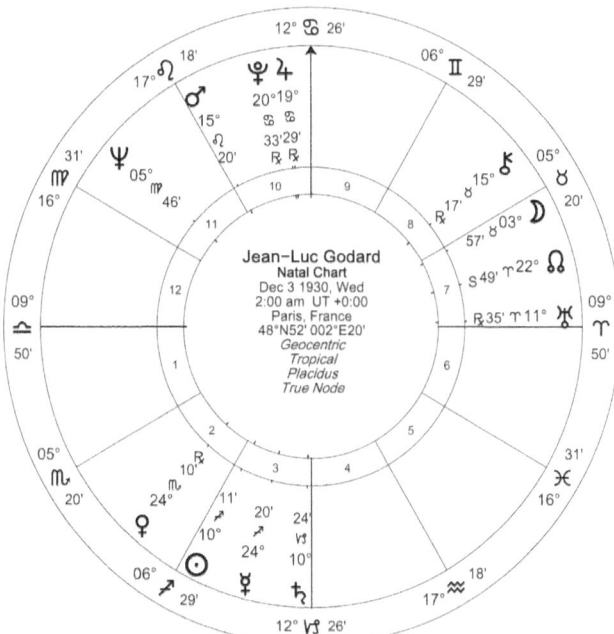

for faith in a Higher power. The third house is related to language, learning and communication. This could indicate an identification (Sun) with moral truths (Sagittarius): "I am a philosopher" or "I am a judge". One's personal philosophy could relate to language and communication (third). The Sun disposes[5] Mars, which is in the tenth. Mars reflects our capacity for assertion and need for freedom. The tenth house is associated with career, success, and authority figures. The Sun is significator of the eleventh house, which is associated with emancipation and causes. This could indicate an intention (Sun) to expand one's influence (Sagittarius) via communications for the sake of human progress (Sun significator of eleventh). The Sun is disposed by Jupiter[6] in Cancer in the tenth. Jupiter represents our ultimate truth. Cancer is associated with family, memory and history. It could indicate that the expression of personal truths (Sun Sagittarius) will be further advanced by theories related to history (Jupiter Cancer).

Neptune in Godard's chart is in Virgo in the eleventh house and signifies the sixth house, which is archetypally associated with Virgo. Virgo represents the need to be competent and of service, to analyze and solve problems. This could suggest an inspiration (Neptune) to serve (Virgo) the cause of societal change (eleventh). In its association with imagination and fantasy, Neptune represents the cinema: in Godard's case, this might be analytical cinema that addresses societal problems.

The *opening* square between the Sun and Neptune in Godard's chart suggests that expression of moral truths (Sun Sagittarius) is perceived as mutually exclusive to the ideal of sacrifice and service to the collective (Neptune Virgo). Partaking in collective dreams requires the sacrifice of personal identity. Therefore, personal creativity in the service of truth (Sun/Sagittarius) could be felt as conflicting with the Neptunian ideal of selfless service (Virgo) to the collective (eleventh). The originating cognition can be expressed as: "My will to find meaning and tell the truth is problematic and may cause suffering to others. Either free will is wrong or its merely an illusion." The result may be irrational guilt leading to various acts of self-undoing.

Initially, this Sun-Neptune psychological dynamics would be mirrored in early childhood experiences that may involve a lack of adequate validation. The originally constructed sense of self may be confused and the person may exhibit low self-esteem. Analogous situations requiring validation of identity will be recreated in an attempt to disconfirm the negative belief and further integrate the aspect.

Archetypally, the Sun represents the father figure as first playmate. The challenging Sun-Neptune dynamic in Godard's chart suggests a father wounded in his self-esteem and who perhaps has over-inflated opinions. Unlike his wife, Godard's father, Paul, did not belong to the "high" Protestant society, and this may have damaged Paul's self-confidence. He was often irritated by and overtly disparaging of Jean-Luc's balancing on chairs, peering over his glasses, or incessant punning. Puns imply the holding in suspension of two conflicting patterns of meaning so that a new emphasis appears. Puns may have reflected Godard's need to construct meaning, a form of creativity that was not applauded by his father, but rather mocked and censured[7].

Godard was not allowed to speak at the table unless he quoted someone else's opinion related to the subject of discussion; if disobedient, he had to eat alone in the kitchen as punishment. Identifying with someone else's "truths" was encouraged at the expense of originality and authenticity of personal opinions. Arts and culture were strongly emphasized in Godard's upbringing, but not cinema. Cinema was dismissed and the subject was forbidden, just like Jean-Luc's opinions.

Godard's family dynamics seems to reflect the conflict (square) between differentiated individuality (Sun) and blissful "oneness" (Neptune). On one hand, his protestant upbringing placed strong emphasis on individual independence. On the other, the extended family on mother's side[8] evoked the fantasy to belong to "an idyllic world of gods and goddesses."[xxii] For Godard, partaking in this magical world necessitated a loss of individuality, a denial of originality, and wearing a mask. Behind the mask was an impostor who felt undeserving of his destiny.

The aolar age in Godard's chart corresponds to 5.4 years (1936). According to the DAM, significant events reflective of the level of integration of the Solar archetype may have occurred at this age[9]. In his Mars planetary age of 64.4 years (1995), Godard released the documentary "JLG/JLG: Self-portrait in December"—a profound self-reflection on his identity.[10] In this documentary, Godard repeatedly refers to an image of himself as a boy at the age of 6 and wonders why he appears so somber: "I was already in mourning for myself, my soul companion, and I suspected that the soul had stumbled on the body and that it had left again without offering its hand."[xxiii] He speculates that this was an unconscious mourning for victims to be in WWII concentration camps. In the ensuing years, the Holocaust would be fully underway. His Sun-Neptune dynamics at age of 6 seem to reflect Godard's psychic attunement to the collective unconscious as well as an intuitive understanding of suffering; that is, suffering that overwhelms the self and induces guilt.

The Holocaust and his Leo developmental stage of 14-20:

> When [it] happened, I was 15 years old. My parents kept it a secret from me, despite belonging to the Red Cross. I only found out about it much later.[xxiv]

The anti-Semitic and anti-war family background of his parents must have exacerbated his guilt: "Even today I still feel guilty . . . I am sorry I couldn't stand up for them."[xxv]

In his Leo developmental stage, which is associated with the consolidation of identity and separation from the family matrix, Godard produced a family pamphlet: "The Family Circle: Overall Impressions," which was an elaborate play of self-signification[xxvi]. The front page was signed with his nickname IAM and moi-meme (myself). The back cover read "Off with the masks." It was indicative of Godard's intention to also drop his mask and separate from this "too much loved and seductive world"[xxvii]. Unconscious guilt associated with the will to differentiate led to destructive acts of self-undoing: procrastinating and failing school exams, dropping out his studies in anthropology, and engaging in regular petty theft from family members. Following a theft from his employer in 1952, Godard's repressed identity (Sun) became a prison and a mental hospital (Neptune) on the outside, for he was temporarily required to be hospitalized as a means to avoid conviction and actual prison.[11] Godard considered his criminal behavior as an expression of his need to become a fully-fledged decision-making agent: "What I wanted was . . . to spend it as I liked"[xxviii].

Following his release from the hospital, it was time for Godard to transform the Neptunian feeling of loss and confusion into inspiration, to identify his dreams, to substantiate them, to prove himself deserving to belong to the elevated world of "gods and goddesses" on his own terms.

The imaginal world of cinema offered the answer. The magazine "Des Cahiers du Cinema"[12] and the circle of artists constituting the French "New Wave" provided a platform for the creative expression of Godard's philosophy regarding the purpose of cinema and filmmakers.

Des Cahiers du Cinema and the French New Wave

Godard's new identity was born in a conservative society that was not conducive to new ideas or artists. For Godard, the cine-clubs of Paris reflected the eleventh house milieu of groups of like-minded colleagues and associates. There Godard encountered "allies" who, like him, were cripplingly shy, had problems with the law, or were academic drop-outs. They were equally addicted to cinema, which Godard defined as "the wall we had to scale to escape from our lives."[xxix] Substituting reality for fantasy seems to have induced a false sense of omnipotence and an over-inflated sense of self-importance.

To define themselves against the existing establishment, the writers for "Des Cahiers du Cinema" operated like a revolutionary "cell" with a utopian political program by promoting an educated taste to improve cinema and thus the world. For Godard[xxx], there was no difference between reality and cinema, between documentary and fiction. By creating movies, film directors created reality. This idea was further supported by the elaborated "politique des auteurs," elevating film directors to the status of great artists, solely responsible for the style and meaning of the film[xxxi]: "A director is as alone on the film-set as the writer before the blank page"[xxxii] and he could express his vision by finding the most appropriate articulation (camera or editing) when filming this reality. The audience was expected to participate in the co-creation of meaning. Therefore, the audience had to be put at a psychological and emotional distance instead of being lured into identifying with the narrative.

It seems that Godard's emerging philosophy about the role of both film-making and film-makers reflected an unconscious fear (square) of the Neptunian imperative to dissolve and render irrelevant any volition or creative self-expression (Sun). Therefore, his threatened "identity" overcompensated by constructing an inflated, narcissistic theory about the film director as God-like creator exercising unchallenged volition. His relationship with the intentionally alienated audience would test whether the reality presented by the director could be trusted by others. Godard's films would replace the Neptunian defense of fantasy, enabling the audience to rise to the level of the director and thus fulfill the director's less conscious need for self-importance (the "New Wave" cinema). His movies (Neptune) would function as a way of verifying whether his creative vision, e.g. truth about reality (Sun), was acceptable (square).

Godard's film *Breathless* (1959) made him the frontrunner of the French "New Wave." It was an incredible success, which over the next decade would be repeated only occasionally. With *Breathless*, Godard dismantled the language (third house) of cinema, revolutionized editing and broke with the classical construction of narrative by introducing false matching shots and jump cuts[13]. His improvisational style went as far as to expect the actors to receive their lines only on the set. There were no rules, or in his words: "I believe a film should have a beginning, a middle and an end, but not necessarily in that order." The abundant use of quotations in his films became a source of creative self-expression as: "It's not where you take things from, it's where you take them to."

A square between yang (Sun) and yin (Neptune) planets can manifest as an alternation between repression and acting out of emotions. During this period, he was described as shy, alone, withdrawn, particularly secretive and enigmatic, but also arrogant, uncompromising, and vicious. Undeniably, however, he was primarily recognized as a genius, a guru whose rules no one dared to oppose.

During this period, Godard was strongly influenced by the existentialism of Sartre and the absurdism of Camus. Existentialism emphasizes individual freedom and defines free will as a responsibility[14]. Absurdism postulates that there is no meaning in the world other than the one we construct ourselves.

The Sun-Neptune dynamics in Godard's chart could indicate that any consciously appropriated belief system could be problematic. His movies from this period demonstrate this, for his characters claim free will as a responsibility, but their free will turns out to be an illusion. In *My Life to Live* (1962), a drama about a young woman who dreams of becoming an actress but slips into prostitution instead, Nana claims responsibility for her choices: "I raise my hand—I am responsible! I smoke—I am responsible! I am unhappy—I am responsible!" At the same time, becoming a prostitute equals the loss (square) of her free will (Sun), for she becomes merely a plaything for others. The film is full of uncanny, mysterious connections and premonitions that turn Nana's death into a formal necessity[xxxiii]. When interrogated by the police for theft and asked what she will do next, Nana answers: "I don't know. 'I' is someone else". Godard demonstrates how the inability to contain and balance the conscious and unconscious parts of the psyche may lead to unconsciously motivated acts of self-undoing and ultimately death. Clearly, this film is largely auto-biographical.

Toward the end of the 1960s, the unprecedented censure of the Gaullist regime and the war in Vietnam shifted Godard's interest from the individual to social systems and the collective unconscious. The individual was perceived as having lost his life purpose, and as performing self-deception or "bad faith "to avoid existential "anguish." Man (Sun) became addicted for his sense of meaning (Sagittarius) to existing societal norms promoting a culture of consumerism and selling illusions (square Neptune).

In *Two or Three Things I Know About Her* (1967), a movie-essay treating the vicissitudes of human existence, the sequence of a cosmos in a coffee cup reads:

> "Perhaps it will make it possible to link up, to move . . . from living in society to living together. But then . . . since I never stop finding myself guilty, even though I feel innocent, since every event transforms my daily life, since I always seem to fail to communicate. . . . Since . . . I can't tear myself away from the objectivity that crushes me, nor from the subjectivity that isolates me, since it isn't possible for me either to raise myself into Being, or to fall into Nothingness . . . it's necessary that I listen . . . that I look around me more than ever . . . the world . . . my fellow creatures . . . my brothers.[xxxiv]

Godard reveals a new expression of his Sun-Neptune dynamics by posing the question of how the individual can belong to the collective without dissolving into it or exhibiting guilt for acting upon his free will. For Godard, the answer was film-making, inciting revolt against the illusions of the enslaving neo-liberalism, and promoting new ideals for containing the interests of the individual within society.

In *Weekend* (1968), an apocalyptic film about a society in which moral responsibility does not exist and self-interest predominates, the end credits include this enigmatic statement: "The end of cinema." It prefigures the upcoming reinvention of Godard as a political activist, a teacher of Marxist philosophy and Maoism, who brooks no interference when lecturing his audience with his films[xxxv]

The Dziga Vertov Group

In 1968, Godard co-founded with Jean-Pierre Gorin the Dziga Vertov Group. The collective was inspired by Marxist ideology, asserting that communism is the historical moment at which individual subjectivity (Sun) and the societal whole (Neptune) could be brought into a transparent and productive relationship (square). They made "political films politically" and without authorship. These are almost unwatchable militant films, meant to provoke political discussion among the viewers. The camera was used as a scalpel and a weapon to brutalize the audience by daring them to make sense out of an inchoate jumble of words and images, scraps of music, and political diatribes.[xxxvi]

It seems that during this period Godard expanded his egoic boundaries by identifying with the whole of society. His higher truth became a Neptunian/Utopian ideology meant to save the lost victims of consumerist society. The Neptunian defense of denial was utilized for the purpose of avoiding the painful truth that many of his movies were neither commercially successful nor widely popular. He projected his own disillusionment onto abstract societal victims and engaged in self-destructive saviour-victim dynamics fuelled by irrational guilt where "saviours" feel compelled to rescue "victims" from the natural consequences of their own self-defeating actions[xxxvii]. Again, Godard was substituting fantasy for reality for the purpose of narcissistic self-aggrandizement. The overextended intention to shape the individual's vision led to totalitarian dominance of the audience, leaving no place for free will. The ultimate resolution was compassion fatigue: burnout for the savior, [figurative] death for the victim.[xxxviii]

All is well (1972), the last and most pessimistic film of the Dziga Vertov group, implied that even leftwing idealism cannot prevent the descent of modern society into soulless consumerism. Godard and Gorin had to accept that their works did not attract sizable audiences and were commercial failures. During this period, the irreverent and arrogant dogmatic style of Godard led to the breakup of the relationship with his friend Francois Truffaut. After Godard asked for financial support with the words: "You have to help me so the public does not get the idea that we all make films like you," Truffaut replied: "Here you are in 1973 . . . as arrogant and dogmatic as ever, secure on your pedestal, indifferent to others. . . . Between your interest in the masses and your own narcissism, there is no room for anything or anyone else".[xxxix]

The Cosmic Period and "Histor(ies) of Cinema"

Godard's next period (1980s-90s) was profoundly melancholic and introspective. The works he made during this period inspire self-reflection and a conscious choice (Sun) to look "inside" (square) and search "beyond" (Neptune) for an answer as to how individuality can exist in the universe or how an individual can relate to God. Neptune transmutes ideology into cosmology.

Godard asserted that our identity (Sun) and conflicts are reflected in and mediated (square) through images (Neptune). In order to identify ourselves in the chain of images, we need to compare images from the "unknown" elsewhere to images from the "known" here. In *Here and Elsewhere* (1976), Godard compares fragments of revolutionary scenes of "elsewhere" (Palestine) with the footage of "here" (France). He lists a series of binary pairs: "here and elsewhere, victory and defeat . . . interior and exterior . . . dream and reality" and adds: "All or nothing, always or never, live or die . . . too simple and too easy to divide the world into two." This contrast stressing the relevance of the conjunction "and" indicates a new evolved paradigm regarding the question of identity. Fixed boundaries should be loosened to become a line of flight that is continually crossed in the ongoing process of identification.[xl] This seems to be a declaration of a willingness to let go of attachments, to sacrifice a fixed identity, and to expand the boundaries of the self. He refers to himself as a "walking network" and "fraction in a world of whole numbers"[xli] and states:

> "I believe I come from elsewhere, let's say space. I have a need to go to Earth. There's something of mine. There is an image I have to uncover, and cinema allows me to do so. Movies are like clouds that sit over reality: if I do cinema well, I can uncover what is beneath, my friends, my allies, what I am, where I come from. Others can't do it. It's too heavy for them. But it's not too heavy for me, because I come from elsewhere."[xlii]

Other themes of this period are the reinstatement of faith in the divine structure of all events on earth, the reaffirmation of the centrality of God in matters of daily existence, the mystery of creation, the meaning of ego-sacrifice, and the alignment of our will with the Divine. In *Hail, Mary!* (1985), a modern version of the story of Joseph and Mary, Godard asserts: "Life was willed, anticipated, organised, and planned in universe" and "Our free will should not be expanded by force, but recovered in oneness from level to level to eternity." The notorious final close up of Mary's open mouth symbolizes to me the opening to mysteries (Neptune) greater than us (Sun) by looking inside of ourselves as we contain and mirror them (square).

During this period, Godard exhibited great interest in human suffering, which he defines as "the most intimate knowledge one can have of oneself, beyond identity."[xliii] Godard suggests that "cinema perhaps has role to play as a depositary, or a guardian of suffering," a place where we can transcend ourselves, learn compassion, and alleviate guilt.

At his Jupiter age of 56.2 years, he started working on a video project, *Histor(ies) of Cinema* (1987-1998), which reflects Jupiter's placement in Cancer (history). Godard is not only the film-maker philosopher, but also an archivist and historian of cinema.[15] His intention is to find answers about his life-purpose by looking into his place in the history of cinema, or thinking of himself "historically." Self-transcendence is sought by claiming sainthood through self-canonisation in the cinematic/human annals.

These films are a kind of elegy for the decline of cinematography resulting from the betrayal of its documentary power and thus the failure to adequately present and confront the Holocaust. For Godard, the documentary function of cinema implies anticipation and bearing witness. Cinema is a kind of clairvoyant that "shows illnesses before they become visible"[xliv]. Besides anticipation, the cinema must bear faithful witness to an ever-changing present.

The image is like evidence in a courtroom. For me, making a movie is like bringing in evidence. The image can be accepted or refused, but it is there for discussion and it awaits a verdict. The very idea of montage is the scales of justice."[xlv]

For Godard, montage involves bringing together (square) fragmented images (Neptune/Virgo) in order to create new meaning (Sun/Sagittarius) in support of cinema's predictive and "curing" function. Godard justifies this by the rapprochement of the terms "Jew" and "Muslim." Prisoners in the concentration camps in the final stages of starvation, exhaustion, and despair were called "Muselmänner." He claims that if concentration camps had been filmed at the time, this usage of the word could have been perceived as an anticipatory indicator of the subsequent conflict in the Middle East.

These films are clear evidence of Godard's attempt to atone for his irrational, unconscious guilt about the Holocaust. He believed that if filmed at the time, the "reality" of the Holocaust would have not been replaced with the Hollywood "fantasy" about it. In the *Histor(ies) of Cinema*, Godard was the judge who found that European cinema had committed a crime of omission and Hollywood a crime of commission. While he sees partial atonement for European cinema in Italian postwar Neorealism, there is no redemption for Hollywood for falsifying European history.[16]

In his Neptune planetary age of 72.6 years, Godard produced a film fragment about time: *Ten minutes older: the Celo* (2002). It gives substance and identity to endings, dissolution, suffering, and the impossibility of love. It is a succinct and brilliant diachronistic reflection of the level of integration of his Sun-Neptune dynamics. Under the subtitle "Last minutes of fear," Godard reveals self-acceptance in an attempt to assuage his existential guilt:

> "I don't know what will be after. I do not want to and I cannot know it. But if it is my wish, if I want to be famous, if I want glory, if I want to be loved by people . . . yet I am not guilty to wish for it, to desire only that!"[xlvi]

Under the title *The Unspeakable*, he revealed documentary images of the Holocaust, the only moments in which the music stops, frozen fractions of time as reparation of guilt on behalf of the collective for the tragic events that he unconsciously sensed at the age of six (Sun) and was unable to prevent. This was an act of redemption for the crime of omission.

Conclusions

My research was intended to answer the question of whether Godard was able to redefine himself and change his personal narrative through an ever-evolving integration of the Sun-Neptune subplot in his chart. My answer is, he did—by inventing the "plotless cinema" in which he was present, almost visible as the director behind his films. He abandoned narrative in favour of an expanded interior, reciprocal dialogue between film maker and audience. As he admits: "I tried to . . . tell a story. But it is not in my nature. . . . . I want to mix everything, to restore everything, to tell everything at the same time"[xlvii]. Thus he himself became the plot of his films. Through his unique eclectic cinema—a mixture of images, texts, sounds, noise, and silence—he constantly redefined himself by reinventing his own "truth."

His "self" as a series of multiple performed roles of "I"s was constructed in the exploration of personal illusions, political ideals, and divine mysteries. It ranged from the self-aggrandizement of the "politique des auteurs" and the dogmatic overextension of the Dziga Vertov group to the deep mytho-poetic self-reflection and increased awareness of individuals as "fractions" in the world of "whole numbers."

In the opening credits of *My Life to Live*, a quote by Montagne reads: "Lend yourself to others and give yourself to yourself." I believe it succinctly reflects the imperative of an integrated Sun-square-Neptune aspect. Only an authentic and self-owned "Self" can appropriate the overwhelming transpersonal dimension of the psyche. Only then is meaningful sacrifice, surrender, humility, and trust in a Higher Power possible.

At his solar age of 5.4 years, Godard, overwhelmed with existential guilt, was struggling to exhibit self-confidence in a world overshadowed by loss and suffering. His volition felt wrong, his identity unseen, his life undeserved. At his Neptune age of 72.6, Godard accepted his will to feel "special" without guilt or fear as to whether this can happen. Over the years, he gradually embodied his personal imperative for "specialness"—the "specialness" that necessitates a conscious choice of self-sacrifice; the "specialness" of becoming a channel of divine love; the "specialness" of feeling "special" in the all-embracing, indiscriminate "whole" of humankind.

I love. There is a promise. I have to sacrifice myself so that through me love's word makes sense. The reward for this long enterprise: I shall all become the one who loves. Thus I shall at least deserve the name I gave myself: A man. Nothing more than a man. No better than any other, but no other better than him.—Jean-Luc Godard

Endnotes

[1] AstroPsychology is a meta-model that synthesizes a variety of ideas from different perspectives, including psychodynamic, cognitive behavioural, Jungian/archetypal, object relations, humanistic, transpersonal, and general systems theory. Furthermore, it employs information derived from developmental psychology and different spiritual traditions that stress the evolution of soul within an overarching, reincarnational framework.

[2] In this research I apply margin of one year before or after the exact planetary age.

[3] According to G. Perry (2013), Narcissistic Personality Disorder (NPD) as solar pathology implies a rigid focus on solar needs, an extreme and excessive manifestation of narcissistic traits as a defense against perceived threats to the solar archetype, resulting in distress and impairment.

[4] The New Wave is a term coined by critics for a group of French filmmakers in the late 1950s and 1960s, such as Francois Truffault, Jacque Rivette, Maurice Sherer, and Godard, who were linked by their appreciation of the American films-noir of Hawks and Hitchcock, Italian neo-realism, the philosophy of existentialism, the politics of auteurs, experimenting with editing, visual style, and narrative as a rebellion against established paradigms of film making.

[5] A dispositor is the planet that rules the sign that another planet occupies. Mars is in Leo, thus Sun as the ruler of Leo disposes Mars. Mars as the disposed planet would provide the background motivation of the Sun as dispositor.

[6] Jupiter as dispositor of the Sun seeks to promote the Sun's agenda and act on the Sun's behalf. It is perhaps relevant that Jupiter Cancer in the 10th is conjunct Pluto, and that Pluto is associated with danger. Pluto widely opposes Saturn Capricorn conjunct IC, which is associated with restrictions. This could indicate opinions and beliefs (Jupiter) that are perceived as dangerous and subject to criticism and censorship both in the family and career environment (Cancer-Capricorn dynamics).

[7] This dynamic is additionally reflected by the placement of Saturn in his chart. Saturn represents father as authority. Saturn Capricorn opposes Jupiter-Pluto in Cancer.
[8] Godard's mother Odile was from the rich and prestigious family of Monod, daughter of Julien Monod, the founder of the Banque Paribas.
[9] The reference to the integration of the solar archetype includes as well the solar aspects, especially Sun square Neptune.
[10] Recall that Mars is disposed by the Sun and provides the background motivation for the Sun to "will," "identify," and "creatively self-express."
[11] Godard's father helped Godard escape charges by transferring him temporarily to a mental hospital.
[12] Established in 1951, this is the most influential French film magazine. It reinvented the basic tenets of film criticism and theory.
[13] These techniques are meant to advance the action. It reflects the Sun as dispositor of Mars, which is associated with improvisation and spontaneity. Furthermore, it could be associated with the prominent placement of Uranus in Godard's chart as a focal point of a T-square to Saturn and Jupiter/Pluto as well as part of a trine with Mars and the Sun.
[14] In terms of astrological archetypes, existentialism can be seen as a blend of Mars/Aries with its emphasis on "existence before essence," implying a world in which "man is freedom," and Saturn/Capricorn as regards the idea that free will is responsibility—not only personal, but for all humankind. With the Sun as dispositor of Mars and the strong emphasis on Saturn in his chart, I find it unsurprising that Godard was influenced by existentialism.
[15] Recall that Jupiter is dispositor of the Sun and therefore would seek to advance the Solar agenda in the resolution of the conflicts associated with the Solar archetype in Godard's chart, including Sun-Neptune dynamics. Jupiter is in Cancer, which relates to history and the past.
[16] In 2002, Godard was awarded an Oscar that he refused to accept, one of the reasons being his disrespect of Spielberg's "Schindler's List," the crime of which was to turn a real-life drama into "une histoire de Hollywood." https://www.theguardian.com/film/2000/feb/11/culture.features

Reference Notes

[i] Perry, G. (2012). *An Introduction to AstroPsychology.* East Hampton, CT: APA Press, pp.310-311.

[ii] Perry, G. (2005). *What is AstroPsychology?* http://aaperry.com/what-is-astropsychology/.

[iii] Perry, G. (2015). *The Developmental Age Method.* Unpublished manuscript as per Grant, J. (2016). *Using the Developmental Age Method to Interpret Significant Experiences in the Lives of Winston Churchill and Franklin Delano Roosevelt.* ISAR International Astrologer, Vol 45 # 1, p.25.

[iv] Perry, G. (2015). *The Developmental Age Method.* Unpublished manuscript as per Grant, J. (2016). *Using the Developmental Age Method to Interpret Significant Experiences in the Lives of Winston Churchill and Franklin Delano Roosevelt.* ISAR International Astrologer, Vol 45 # 1, p.26.

[v] Perry, G. (2012). *The Archetypal Origins of Motivation.* http://aaperry.com/archetypal-motivation/.

[vi] Perry, G. (2011). *The Protean Nature of Astrological Archetypes.* http://aaperry.com/archetypal-astrology/ & Perry, G. (2005). *Astrological Archetypes as Geometric Forms,* http://aaperry.com/astrological-archetypes-as-geometric-forms/

[vii] Perry, G. (2005). *Astrological Archetypes as Geometrical Forms.* http://aaperry.com/astrological-archetypes-as-geometric-forms/ & Perry, G. (2012). *An Introduction to AstroPsychology.* East Hampton, CT: APA Press, pp.7, 14.

[viii] Perry, G. (2012). *From Royalty to Revolution.* East Hampton, CT: APA Press, chapter II, p.41.

[ix] Perry, G. (2012). *From Royalty to Revolution.* East Hampton, CT: APA Press, chapter II, p.44.

[x] Perry, G. (2012). *From Royalty to Revolution.* East Hampton, CT: APA Press, chapter II, p.44.

[xi] Perry, G. (2012). *From Royalty to Revolution.* East Hampton, CT: APA Press, chapter II, p.57.

[xii] Perry, G. (2016). *Saturn square Neptune and the Danger of False Narratives.* http://aaperry.com/saturn-square-neptune/

[xiii] Perry, G. (2012). *An Introduction to AstroPsychology.* East Hampton, CT: APA Press, p.288.

[xiv] Perry, G. (2012). *An Introduction to AstroPsychology.* East Hampton, CT: APA Press, p.289.

[xv]Perry, G. (2012). *An Introduction to AstroPsychology.* East Hampton, CT: APA Press, pp.288-290.
[xvi]Perry, G. (2012). *An Introduction to AstroPsychology.* East Hampton, CT: APA Press, p.289.
[xvii]Perry, G. (2006). *Stealing Fire from the Gods.* East Hampton, CT: APA Press, p.101-102.
[xviii]Kowalski, D. *Quietism—The Passive Christian Life.* http://www.apologeticsindex.org/2985-quietism.
[xvix]Wikipedia. *Quietism (Christian philosophy).* https://en.wikipedia.org/wiki/Quietism_(Christian_philosophy)
[xx]De Molinos, M. (1685). *Spiritual Guide.* Venice, part II, chapter XIX.
[xxi]MacCabe, C. (2003). *Godard, a Portrait of the Artist at Seventy.* UK: The Blumsburry Press, p.63.
[xxii]MacCabe, C. (2003). *Godard, a Portrait of the Artist at Seventy.* UK: The Blumsburry Press, p.18.
[xxiii]New Wave Film.com. *Jean-Luc Godard.* http://www.newwavefilm.com/french-new-wave-encyclopedia/jean-luc-godard.shtml, p.18-19.
[xxiv]Buchanan, K. *Jean-Luc Godard says Honorary Oscar meant „Nothing" to him.* http://www.vulture.com/2010/11/jean-luc-godard_says_honorary.html.
[xxv]Buchanan, K. *Jean-Luc Godard says Honorary Oscar meant „Nothing" to him.* http://www.vulture.com/2010/11/jean-luc-godard_says_honorary.html.
[xxvi]MacCabe, C. (2003). *Godard, a Portrait of the Artist at Seventy.* UK: The Blumsburry Press, p.34.
[xxvii]MacCabe, C. (2003). *Godard, a Portrait of the Artist at Seventy.* UK: The Blumsburry Press, chapter I
[xxviii]MacCabe, C. (2003). *Godard, a Portrait of the Artist at Seventy.* UK: The Blumsburry Press, p.3.
[xxix]New Wave Film.com. *Jean-Luc Godard.*http://www.newwavefilm.com/french-new-wave-encyclopedia/jean-luc-godard.shtml, p.2.
[xxx]MacCabe, C. (2003). *Godard, a Portrait of the Artist at Seventy.* UK: The Blumsburry Press, p.72.
[xxxi]MacCabe, C. (2003). *Godard, a Portrait of the Artist at Seventy.* UK: The Blumsburry Press, p.73.
[xxxii]Morrey, D. (2005). *Jean-Luc Godard.* Manchester, UK: Man-

chester University Press, chapter 3.
[xxxiii]Morrey, D. (2005). *Jean-Luc Godard*. Manchester, UK: Manchester University Press, chapter 3.
[xxxiv]Dixon, W. *The Films of Jean-Luc Godard*. Albany, NY: State University of New York Press, p.76.
[xxxv]Dixon, W. *The Films of Jean-Luc Godard*. Albany, NY: State University of New York Press, p.88.
[xxxvi]Dixon, W. *The Films of Jean-Luc Godard*. Albany, NY: State University of New York Press, p.91.
[xxxvii]Perry, G. (2016). *Saturn square Neptune and the Danger of False Narratives*. http://aaperry.com/saturn-square-neptune/ & Perry, G. (2012). *An Introduction to AstroPsychology*. East Hampton, CT: APA Press, pp. 173-176.
[xxxviii]Ibid.
[xxxix]MacCabe, C. (2003). *Godard, a Portrait of the Artist at Seventy*. UK: The Blumsburry Press, p.273.
[xl]Morrey, D. (2005). *Jean-Luc Godard*. Manchester, UK: Manchester University Press, p.108.
[xli]Morrey, D. (2005). *Jean-Luc Godard*. Manchester, UK: Manchester University Press, p.153.
[xlii]Dixon, W. *The Films of Jean-Luc Godard*. Albany, NY: State University of New York Press, p.178.
[xliii]Morrey, D. (2005). *Jean-Luc Godard*. Manchester, UK: Manchester University Press, p.143.
[xliv]Witt, M. (2013). *Jean-Luc Godard, Cinema Historian*. Bloomington, Indiana: Indiana University Press, p.124.
[xlv]Witt, M. (2013). *Jean-Luc Godard, Cinema Historian*. Bloomington, Indiana: Indiana University Press, p.126.
[xlvi]Godard, Jean-Luc (2012). *In the Darkness of Time. Ten minutes older: The Celo*. http://www.bing.com/videos/search?q=youtube+godard+ten+minutes+older+the+celo&view=detail&mid=F1B055B899F1851AABE5F1B055B899F1851AABE5&FORM=VIRE.
[xlvii]Dixon, W. *The Films of Jean-Luc Godard*. Albany, NY: State University of New York Press, p.73.

Predicting Weather with Astrology

By Alphee Lavoie

ABSTRACT: Can we predict weather for a certain locality using astrology? There is a long history of astrology and weather prediction. Astrologers Johannes Kepler and A .J. Pearce have claimed that astrological signs, houses, and aspects can produce wet weather and others can bring sunshine, cold weather, lightning storm, etc. Some of these astrologers were more into predicting long weather trends by using the aspects between slow moving planets from Jupiter on. Benjamin Franklin is a well-known person in United States history but was not well known as an astrologer. He predicted the weather beginning in 1732 and for years following using astrology in his publication *Poor Richard's Almanack*. In 1949, C. C. Zain wrote a book on predicting weekly weather.

Introduction

This research will attempt to determine the accuracy of the method of weather prediction described in the Church of Light book *Weather Predicting* by C. C. Zain. He predicted weekly weather using planetary positions in signs and houses and also the angular differences between the planets on the ecliptic, known to astrologers as aspects. According to his book, by calculating each Quarter Moon for each month of the year for a specific locality he was able to predict what the weather would be for that locality for each week. According to Zain, by studying the different astrological criteria of the planets in those Quarter Mmoon charts, he could predict if the temperature would be hot or cold, if it would be rainy or dry and sunny, if there would be the possibility of lightning storms, and much more. C. C. Zain found the signs that the Moon and its dispositor are in are both extremely important in predicting the weather. He also found that the signs on the cusp of the IC and the Ascendant and their rulers are important, as well as the house placements of those rulers.

In his book Zain assigned weights to certain parts of the Quarter Moon chart, finding that certain parts had more and less influence on the result. He claims that the fourth house, including the sign on the cusp, the planets in the fourth, and aspects they make account for 50 percent of the influence on the weather. He would also analyze the dispositor of the planet ruling the fourth house cusp. He found that the first house (Ascendant), the sign on the first house cusp, the ruler of the cusp, and planets in the first house have a 25 percent influence on the weather. The final 25 percent of the weather influence comes from planets in angles and the astrological sign that the Moon is in. The Moon's dispositor and house location are also extremely important in predicting the weather. So it comes down to: Ascendant, fourth house, planets in angles, and the Moon. Analyzing these, you should be able to accurately predict what the weather will be for the next week.

Methodology

A dataset for 80 years of weather for Hartford, Connecticut was created with a coding system that could be used to research specific weather conditions. Quarter Moon charts for each month for 80 years were calculated, with the chart title containing the code assigned in the database that corresponded to the weather description for that Quarter Moon period. The coding and program allowed multiple conditions,(e.g., cold and wet) and singular conditions)e.g., warm(. Conditions could be combined so that both uppercase K and uppercase S could be used to research all the Quarters of the Moon that had two to three inches of rain with a temperature that was below average for three or more days in that week.

The Coding List

Key	Short Description	Detailed Description
A	Lots of Sunshine	85-100% sunny
B	Average Sunshine	41-85% sunny
C	Wind 25+	Wind gust 25 mph, one or more occurrence
D	Wind 30+	Wind gust 30 mph, one or more occurrence
E	1-3 snow	1-3" of snow, single occurrence
F	3-6 snow	3-6" of snow, single occurrence
G	6-12 snow	6-12" of snow, single occurrence
H	12+ snow	12+" of snow, single occurrence
I	0-1 rain	0-1" of rain, single occurrence
J	1-2 rain	1-2" of rain, single occurrence
K	2-3 rain	2-3" of rain, single occurrence
L	3+	3+" of rain, single occurrence
M	Heavy Fog	one or more occurrence of heavy fog
N	Lightning	one or more occurrence of thunder

O	Hail	One or more occurrence of hail
P	Temp above 90	One or more occurrence of above 90 temperature
Q	Temp below zero	One or more occurrence of below 0 temperature
R	High of the month	3 or more days above average temperature
S	Low of the month	3 or more days below average temperature
T	Hardly any sun	40% or less sun
U	Consecutive dry days	5 or more consecutive days with no precipitation
V	Not used	
W	Days consecutive rain	3 or more consecutive days of rain
X	Total precipitation > 3 inches	3+" of rain during cycle
Y	Total precipitation > 4 inches	4+" of rain during cycle
Z	Not used	

Moon Phases

A	New Moon
B	1st Quarter Moon
C	Full Moon
D	3rd Quarter

Season

E	Spring
F	Summer
G	Fall
H	Winter

AIR Software's Fast Research Program was used to do the research. The program allows the creation of predictive models of astrological criteria to test each method in Zain's book. Anything in the sky that moves is included in Fast Research and can be included in the models. Using these astrological models, the chi-square and probability of each criterion in

the models was tested against a control group. This methodology is based on pure scientific research techniques.

Results

1. Zain claims that the wettest planets are the Moon, Venus, and Saturn.

- 3 to 12+ inches of snow: Venus in first house with a high chi-square (20), probability 99%.
- Often.
- 1 to 3+ inches of rain: Venus (chi-square 2.3) and Saturn (chi-square 3.1) in first house. Often.
- 3 or more consecutive days of rain: Venus in the first house (chi-square 6.2), probability 98.6. Often.
- 3 or more consecutive days of rain: Venus in the Ascendant and in the fourth house as a chi-square of 3.3, probability 92.9%. Often.
- 3 or more inches of rain: Moon in the first house (chi-square 6.8), probability 99.8%. Often.
- 3 or more inches of rain: Moon in the first house or fourth house)chi-square 14.2), probability
- 100%. Often.
- 3 or more inches of rain: Moon, Venus, Saturn in an angular house has a high probability (over 90%). Often.

Conclusion: Zain's findings seem to work very well. Venus has the highest probability to bring rain when it is angular, followed by Saturn and then the Moon.

2. Zain claims that the wet signs are Capricorn, Scorpio, Cancer, Pisces, and Taurus, in that order.

Results:

- Moon, Ascendant, and IC in air signs have a probability of 97.4% dry. Often.
- Moon, IC, and Ascendant in water signs have a probability of 99.1% for rain. Often.

3 To 12 Inches of Snow:

- Moon in water sign (chi-square 8.2), probability 98.6%. Often.
- IC in water sign (chi-square 2.5), probability 88.5%. Often.
- IC in the sign of Scorpio, probability 100%. Often.
- Ascendant in Scorpio (chi-square 4.7), probability 97%. Often.
- Moon in Scorpio (chi-square 1.5), probability 78.6%. Often.
- Moon in Cancer (chi-square 4.9), probability 97.3%. Often.
- Dispositor of the Ascendant in Capricorn (chi-square 19.7), probability 100%.
- Dispositor of the Ascendant in Pisces (chi-square 19.9), probability 99.9%.
- Dispositor of the IC in Capricorn (chi-square 19.4), probability 100%.
- Dispositor of the Moon in Capricorn (chi-square 3.8), probability 90.5%.
- Dispositor of the Moon in Scorpio (chi-square 5.1), probability 97.7%.
- Dispositor of the Ascendant in Scorpio, probability 100%.

Consecutive days of rain:
- Ascendant and IC in Cancer, probability 89.5%. Often.
- IC in Cancer or Capricorn, probability 84.8 %. Often.
- Moon in Pisces or Scorpio, probability 85%. often.
- Ascendant in Pisces or Scorpio, probability 94%. Often.
- Moon, Ascendant, or IC in Taurus, probability 82%. Often.
- Dispositor of the IC in Cancer (chi-square 12.0), probability 99.9%. Often.
- Dispositor of the Moon in Cancer (chi-square 3.0), probability 91.7%. Often.
- Dispositor of the Ascendant in Scorpio (chi-square 3.2), probability 92.6 %. Often.
- Dispositor of the Moon in Scorpio (chi-square 3.0), probability 91.8%. Often.

2 to 3 inches of rain:
- Moon in water sign (chi-square 6.6), probability 99%. Often.
- Ascendant in water sign (chi-square 1.3), probability 74.3%. Often.
- Moon in Pisces (chi-square 12.5), probability 100%. Often.
- IC in Capricorn (chi-square 3.5), probability 93.7. Often.
- Moon in Pisces or Scorpio, probability 88.3%. Often.
- IC in Cancer or Capricorn, probability 87.1%. Often.

Conclusion: Capricorn and Scorpio are not only wet but also stormy. They seem to bring heavy rain and heavy snow and often floods and blizzards. But you can't leave out the signs of Cancer and Pisces, also very wet signs. But all the water signs in general will bring wet weather.

Some criteria that stood out to bring in wet weather:
- Pluto opposition Ascendant (chi-square 3.7), probability 94.7%. Often.
- Pluto conjunction Moon (chi-square 4.8(, probability 97.2%. Often.
- Neptune conjunction Ascendant (chi-square 3.6), probability 94.3%. Ooften.
- Neptune opposition IC ruler (chi-square 5.4), probability 98%. Often.
- Neptune square IC ruler (chi-square 5.8), probability 98.4%. Often.
- Neptune conjunction IC ruler (chi-square 4.2), probability 96.0%. Often.
- Neptune conjunction Ascendant ruler (chi-square 6.2), probability 98.8%. Often.
- Saturn square Moon (chi-square 4.5), probability 96.7%. Often.
- Saturn conjunction Ascendant (chi-square 7.7), probability 99.4%. Often.
- Uranus conjunction IC ruler (chi-square 4.4), probability 96.3%. Often.
- Uranus conjunction planets in IC (chi-square 2.2), probability 85.7%. Often.
- Uranus opposition IC (chi-square 2.5), probability 88.5%. Often.
- Mars opposition IC (chi-square 4.2), probability 95.9%. Often.
- Mars opposition Ascendant ruler (chi-square 4.6), probability 96.8%. Often.

Conclusion: Notice that the conjunctions and the oppositions to these points happen more often and have a higher probability to bring more wet weather. The planets Uranus, Neptune, and Pluto had the strongest results. Also, I found that Pluto was more tied to the Ascendant and its ruler and Uranus was more tied to the IC and had hardly anything to the Ascendant or its ruler. Neptune was strong to the Ascendant and IC. The research also shows that Venus and Saturn conjunction the Ascendant was high probability to bring rain. Planetary aspects to the Moon position were hardly noticeable. The aspects were more to the Ascendant and the IC, as Zain wrote in his book.

What I loved about this research project was that I found that the easy aspects, the sextile and the trine, aspecting these points had a high probability of no rain. It proves what astrologers have been saying for years. The conjunctions, oppositions, and squares create action and the sextiles and the trines are too lazy to produce results.

3. Zain claims that of the dry signs, Aries and Aquarius are the driest, and then Gemini, Sagittarius, and Leo, in that order.

Results:

Ascendant, IC and Moon in sign:
- IC in Aries (chi-square 6.6), probability 99%. Often.
- IC in Gemini (chi-square 6.4), probability 99%. Often.
- Ascendant in Leo (chi-square 3.5), probability 97.5%. Often
- Moon in Leo (chi-square 6.0), probability 98.6%. Often.
- Moon in Aquarius (chi-square 5.0), probability 97.5%. Often.
- Moon in Virgo (chi-square 4.7), probability 97%. Often.
- Moon in Aquarius (chi-square 2.7), probability 90.2%. Often.

- Moon in Leo (chi-square 2.5), probability 88.5%. Often.
- Moon in fixed signs (chi-square 2.9), probability 91.4%. Often.

Dispositor of the Moon, IC, Ascendant:

- Dispositor of Moon in Virgo (chi-square 14.5), probability 100 %. often.
- Dispositor of Moon in Aries (chi-square 4.9), probability 97.3%. often.
- Dispositor of Ascendant in Leo (chi-square 6.0), probability 98.6%. Often.
- Dispositor of Ascendant in Virgo (chi-square 5.3), probability 97.9%. Often.
- Dispositor of Ascendant in Libra (chi-square 9.7), probability 98.8 %. Often.
- Dispositor of Ascendant in Aries (chi-square 12.4), probability 100%. Often.
- Dispositor of IC in Libra (chi-square 4.6), probability 96.8%. Often.
- Dispositor of IC in Gemini (chi-square 9.5), probability 99.8. Often.
- Dispositor of IC in Virgo (chi-square 12.2), probability 100 %. Often.

Planets aspecting major points:

- Uranus conjunction Ascendant ruler (chi-square 4.3 probability 96.3. Often.
- Uranus conjunction Ascendant (chi-square 5.6), probability 92.2%. Often.
- Uranus trine IC (chi-square 4.9), probability 97.3%. Often.
- Uranus sextile IC (chi-square 3.3), probability 93.1%. Often.

- Uranus conjunction Ascendant ruler (chi-square 5.3), probability 97.8%. Often.
- Mars conjunction IC ruler (chi-square 6.2), probability 98.8. Often.
- Saturn conjunction IC ruler (chi-square 2.5), probability 8.9%. Often.
- Saturn trine IC ruler (chi-square 4.3), probability 96.2%. Often.
- Neptune sextile IC ruler (chi-square 2.5), probability 88.3%. Often.
- Mars trine Ascendant ruler (chi-square 5.1), probability 97.7%. Often.
- Pluto conjunction Ascendant ruler (chi-square 3.2), probability 92.7. Often.
- Pluto sextile IC (chi-square 6.0), probability 98.6%. Seldom.
- Pluto sextile Ascendant ruler (chi-square 6.1), probability 98.7%. Often.

Planets in houses:
- Saturn in tenth house (chi-square 6.3), probability 98.8%. Often.
- Saturn in seventh house (chi-square 2.7), probability 89.8%. Often.
- Uranus in seventh house (chi-square 6.2), probability 98.8%. Often.
- Uranus in tenth house (chi-square 2.5), probability 88.5%. Often.
- Jupiter in tenth house (chi-square 3.3), probability 92.8%. Often.
- Jupiter in seventh house (chi-square 4.1), probability 95.6%. Often.

- Mercury in seventh house (chi-square 4.1), probability 95.7%. Often.
- Pluto in seventh house (chi-square 5.4), probability 98%. Often.
- Mars in tenth house (chi-square 4.3), probability 96.1%. Often.

Conclusion: Our research shows that if any of the important points—IC, Ascendant, Moon, and their dispositors—are in Aries, Gemini, Leo, Virgo, Libra, and Aquarius, the weather tends to be drier. No rain. The signs Virgo, Leo, and Aries are the driest.

The research also shows that the planets we found in the first and the fourth houses of the Quarter Moon chart bring rain. Those same planets in the tenth and seventh houses tend to bring dry weather. It shows that the squares and oppositions to important points bring wet weather and trines and sextiles to these points bring drier weather. The conjunction seems to swing both ways, just as it does in other branches of astrology.

4. Zain claims that the signs of Aquarius and Leo and the planet Uranus all bring electrical storms.

Results:

- Dispositor of Ascendant in Leo (chi-square 14.6), probability 100%. Often.
- Dispositor of Moon in Leo (chi-square 14.2), probability 100%. Often.
- Dispositor of IC in Leo (chi-square 12.1), probability 99.9%. Often.
- Dispositor of IC in Virgo (chi-square 3.3), probability 93.0%. Often.
- Dispositor of IC in Gemini (chi-square 2.2), probability 86.1% . Often.

- Dispositor of Ascendant in Libra (chi-square 2.6), probability 89.1%. Often.
- IC in Aquarius (chi-square 30.5), probability 100%. Often.
- IC in Aries (chi-square 6.6), probability 90.0%. Often.
- IC in air sign (chi-square 2.6), probability 89.1%. Often.
- IC in Capricorn (chi-square 16.7), probability 100%. Often.
- IC in Scorpio (chi-square 5.1), probability 97.7%. Often.
- Ascendant in Leo (chi-square 4.8), probability 97.2. Often.
- Ascendant in Scorpio (chi-square 17.4), probability 100%. Often.
- Moon in Aquarius (chi-square 5.0), probability 97.5%.
- Moon in Leo (chi-square 2.5(, probability 88.5%.
- Moon in air sign (chi-square 3.0), probability 91.8%.
- Sun in the IC (chi-square 95.5), probability 99.8. Often.
- Sun angular (chi-square 42.2), probability 100%. Often.
- Sun intercepted (chi-square 10.6), probability 99.9%. Often.
- Intercepted MC IC (chi-square 30.6), probability 100%. Often.
- Uranus in first house (chi-square 25.5) probability 100%.
- Pluto in first house (chi-square 20.9) probability 100%. Often.
- Uranus conjunction IC (chi-square 4.2) probability 96% often
- Saturn, Venus, Sun, Mercury and Mars on the MC (high chi-square often

Conclusion: Lightning is associated with a lot of planets on the Midheaven of the New Moon chart. Mutable signs on angles seldom bring lightning. The Sun and Uranus seem to be tied with lightning, and also Pluto. Aquarius, Leo, Capricorn, and Scorpio are the strongest signs associated with lightning. Stormy days have a high probability of Scorpio and Capricorn, and the wet section showed a high probability of these signs with downpours and floods. This makes a lot of sense seeing that lightning storms often have downpours and also flooding.

Benjamin Franklin, in his *Poor Richard's Almanack*, claims that Mercury-Saturn aspects bring lightning. My research proves that to be true.

- Mercury conjunction Saturn, 2° orb (chi-square 8.0), probability 99.5%. Often.
- Mercury opposition Saturn, 2° orb (chi-square 8.0), probability 99.5%. Often.
- Mercury conjunct Saturn 3° orb (chi-square 4.5), probability 96.6%. Often.

5. Sunshine; Zain did not postulate about sunshine in his book.

Results:

- Dispositor of Ascendant in Leo (chi-square 44.0), probability 100%.
- Dispositor of Ascendant in Libra chi-square 9.5(, probability 99.8.
- Dispositor of Ascendant in Virgo chi-square 7.2), probability 99.3%. Often.
- Dispositor of IC in Leo (chi-square 4.0), probability 95.5 %.
- Dispositor of IC in Gemini)chi-square 3.9), probability 95.1%. Often.
- Dispositor of IC in Ptolemaic aspects to Uranus (chi-square 5.8), probability 98.4%. Often.

- Dispositor of Moon in Virgo (chi-square 8.0), probability 99%. Often.
- Dispositor of Moon in Taurus (chi-square 6.0), probability 98.6%.
- Dispositor of Moon in Gemini (chi-square 2.2), probability 86.0%.
- IC in Aquarius (chi-square 2.6), probability 89.4%. Often.
- IC in Libra)chi-square 2.1), probability 85.7%. Often.
- Moon in Virgo (chi-square 2.7), probability 90.0 %. Often.
- Moon in Taurus (chi-square 2.1), probability 5.3%. Often.
- Moon in earth sign (chi-square 2.3), probability 87.3% %. Often.
- Moon in Gemini (chi-square 3.3), probability 93.1%. Often.
- Ascendant in earth sign)chi-square 2.2), probability 86.3%. Often.
- Ascendant in Leo (chi-square 4.7), probability 97.0%. Often.
- Ascendant in mutable sign (chi-square), 1.6 probability 79.1%. Ooften.
- Ascendant in fire sign (chi-square 4.9), probability 97.2%. Often.
- Ascendant in Virgo (chi-square 7.6), probability 99.4%. Often.
- Ascendant in Aries)chi-square 6.6), probability 99.0%. Often.
- Ascendant in Taurus (chi-square 3.3), probability 92.9%. Often.
- Moon in fourth house)chi-square 3.3), probability 92.9%. Often.

- Sun in fourth house (chi-square 5.7), probability 98.3%. Often.
- Uranus opposition IC (chi-square 5.6), probability 97.5%. Often.
- Uranus conjunction Ascendant (chi-square 4.0), probability 95.4%. Often.

Conclusion: When the Moon, Ascendant, and dispositor of the Moon are in Virgo there are more sunshine days. This is also true if the Moon is in an earth sign. The Ascendant in a mutable sign or in a fire sign also produces sunshine. The IC in an air sign brings more sunshine. If the Sun and Moon are in the fourth house, it brings more sunshine days. Uranus has a lot to do with sunshine. When Uranus makes an aspect to the Moon, Ascendant, or IC there are more sunny days. If the Moon, Ascendant, or IC and its dispositor are in water signs, there are fewer sunshine days.

6. The time of day you can expect the rain to start.

Results:
- Sun in transiting twelfth house (chi-square 2.1), probability 85.7%. Often.
- Sun in transiting third house (chi-square 89.3), probability 100%. Often.
- Moon in transiting sixth house (chi-square 1.5), probability 78%. Often.
- Sun conjunction IC (chi-square 43.2(, probability 100%. Often.
- Sun sextile transiting Ascendant (chi-square 19.0(, probability 100%. Often.
- Sun square transiting Ascendant (chi-square 9.3), probability 99.8%. Often.
- Sun semisquare transiting Ascendant)chi-square 5.2),

probability 97.7%. Often.
- Moon opposition transiting Ascendant (chi-square 4.5), probability 96.5%. Often.
- Moon sextile transiting Ascendant (chi-square 3.1), probability 92.3%. Often.
- Sun conjunction transiting Ascendant)chi-square 2.1), probability 85.7%. Often.
- Sun trine transiting Ascendant) chi-square 11.8), probability 99.9%. Seldom.
- Sun trine transiting IC (chi-square 2.3), probability 86.7%. Seldom.
- Sun in transiting fifth house (chi-square 17.6), probability 100%. Seldom.
- Sun in transiting angular house)chi-square 10.2), probability 99.9%. Seldom.

Final Summary

The methodology used to predict the weather in *Weather Predicting* by C.C. Zain, published by the Church of Light, proves to be scientifically correct. We are delighted to report that the results of this study were able to duplicate what Zain proposed in his book. This is an important step forward in the use of astrology to predict the weather.

References

AIR Software Fast Research Astrology Program: Lavoie, Alphee and Tarasov, Sergey.

Johannes Kepler (n.d.). in *Wikipedia*. Retrieved July 17, 2016 from http://www.newworldencyclopedia.org/entry/Johannes_Kepler.

Pearce, A.J. *The Textbook of Astrology*, Tempe, AZ, AFA, 2006.

Poor Richard's Almanack, (n.d.). in *Wikipedia*. Retrieved July 17, 2016 from https://en.wikipedia.org/wiki/Poor_Richard%27s_Almanack.

Zain, C. C., Course 15, *Weather Predicting*, The Hermetic System of Astrological Weather

Analysis. Albuquerque, NM, Church of Light, 2011.

Nergal
The Shaping of the God Mars in Sumer, Assyria, and Babylon

By José Luis Belmonte

ABSTRACT: This paper examines the latest findings about the Babylonian god *Nergal* in the field of Assyriology and history of the Near East, and focuses on different deities that were conflated and syncretized to create a Neo-Babylonian version of the god *Nergal*, as well as the earliest myths, characters, and figures which shaped the attributes of the god. The attributes and characteristics of *Nergal* are used as evidence to show that it was very likely that the planet Mars (Ares in Greek) was syncretized from *Nergal*, and that Mars as ruler of Aries and Scorpio might have been derived from Babylon as well. In general, the goal is to research whether the astrological meaning of each planet that is used in astrology today had its origins in Babylon, not in Greece nor in any Greek or Latin speaking country of antiquity.

Introduction

It is known from the astrology of Hellenistic period that Mars ruled Aries and Scorpio, and was a god of war, death, and plagues. It was just after the discovery of Pluto in 1930 that the rulers of Scorpio were Pluto and Mars, and that Pluto assumed some of the attributes of Mars, such as death and ruler of the underworld. It was in Babylon that the god *Nergal* was associated to the planet Mars. *Nergal* was a god of war, a fighter, a hero, and also a god of death, plague and ruler of underworld. The fact that the Greek Ares and the Roman Mars are so similar to *Nergal* imply not only that they might be a very similar version or a syncretism of Nergal but also that as ruler of Aries and Scorpio, might also come from Babylon.

In *Tetrabiblos* (Book I, 17), Ptolemy wrote that Mars was "assigned Scorpio and Aries, having a similar nature, and, agreeably to Mars' destructive nature and inharmonious quality."[1] At least since the time of Ptolemy Mars was considered the ruler of Aries and Scorpio; however, Ptolemy did not explain the reasons for ruling those astrological signs. The explanation is not to be found in the Greek world of Antiquity when Hellenistic astrology was born but in the neighboring Near Est, in Mesopotamia, the territory of the current Iraq which in the past hosted the Sumerian, Babylonian, and Assyrian empires.

The Meaning of Nergal

Known today as the red planet, Mars is traditionally associated with blood due to the reddish hue of the planet. Like Mars, the brightest star of the constellation of Scorpio, Antares, has also a reddish color. Antares in Greek stands for "equal of Ares" which means equal to Mars. Based on the many names of Mars in Babylon and the names of the constellations associated to it, Ulla Koch-Westenholz argues that Mars in Mesopotamia was sometimes referred to as sa_5 "red," while in others was considered not only bringer of evil but with a sinister character.[2] The Babylonians not only described Mars as a red, but also named the constellation of Scorpio GIR.TAB, which in Akkadian means scorpion and bears certain associations to death as a result from the bite of a scorpion.

In astrological context, the Akkadians called the planet Mars *Salbatānu*, a name which was explained as "constantly portending pestilence" or as "the incalculable star."[3]

In Babylon, the planet *Salbatānu* (Mars) was associated to *Nergal*. From the language perspective, Gwendolyn Leick argues that *Nergal* was not from Sumer but seemed to be a Babylonian god, because the etymology of the name *Nergal*, which was written ᵈGIR.UNU.GAL or ᵈU.GAR, is not Sumerian but Akkadian.[4] However, J.J.M. Roberts argues that *Nergal* was a Sumerian city god of Kutha who was identified by the Akkadians with *Erra*. According to Roberts, the Sumerian name became popular in Akkadian circles and gradually pushed *Erra* into the background in Akkadian texts, a process which may have already be seen in the Sargonid period (722-622 BCE) when Erra was very popular in personal names but replaced from the inscriptions by *Ner(i)gal*.[5] The gods *Nergal* and *Erra* were originally separate entities. However, the two gods went under the name *Nergal* in the first millennium BCE[6]. *Erra*, god of "scorched earth," raids and riots, was syncretized with *Nergal*, god of war, sudden death and ruler of the world of the dead.[7]

Nergal: God of War and Plague

In addition to the underworld, Nergal was associated with fevers, plagues, and forest fires, and had sometimes a warlike aspect, write Jeremy Black and Anthony Green.[8]

Nergal adopted many of the features of Erra, which was not only was a violent warlike god responsible for plagues, but was worshipped at E-meslam.[9] Actually the most characteristic portrayal of *Erra* was as a warrior whose main weapon was famine.

In the Ur III period Nergal was worshipped at a temple located at Kutha called *E-meslam*, which means "Meslam House." The name *Meslamta-ea* means "he who comes out of Emeslam."[10] *Nergal* seemed to have been promoted by the Sargonid kings (c. 2350-2150 BCE), together with his cult centre at Kutha.[11] *Nergal* was first and foremost an important war-god, and was known as the head of Kutha's pantheon from the time of Naram-sin (reigned ca. 2254-2218 BCE) onwards.[12]

The name *Nergal* appeared frequently in cylinder seals, greetings and personal names of the Middle and Neo-Babylonian period; and numerous prayers and hymns were addressed to the god in order to avert his dangerous influence. The hymns speak of Nergal as a warrior, a god of pestilence and disease, and as god of fertility and vegetation. In Assyria, Sargon II (reigned 722-705 BCE) and his descendants worshipped the warrior god *Nergal*.[13]

Therefore, the attributes of Nergal as a warrior and a god of war are thoroughly present in Mesopotamia, in different periods.

Nergal as an Underworld Deity

Nergal was a major netherworld god from the Old Babylonian period (second millennium BCE) onwards.[14] The following two myths explained the connection between *Nergal* and the netherworld: the first myth, known as "Enlil and Ninlil" and reconstructed from tablets dating from the Old and Middle-Babylonian period, plus a Neo-Assyrian copy, explained how Nergal was originally born as a deity of the netherworld. In the myth,[15] the god Enlil assumed three different forms to copulate with his wife Ninlil. As a result, three gods of the netherworld were conceived.[16] One of these was Nergal.

The second myth, known as "Nergal and Ereshkigal," has come down to us in two versions: the earlier one, from the fourteen century BCE, was found in Tell el-Amarna in Egypt, the later version is from two libraries of the first millennium BCE, one is Neo-Assyrian from Sultantepe of the seventh century BCE (or late eight century BCE), and the other is Late Babylonian from Uruk of the fourth century BCE.[17] Both versions described how Nergal became king of the Netherworld by marrying Ereshkigal, the queen of the Netherworld.

According to Dina Katz, beginning in the Old Babylonian period the status of Nergal in the netherworld prevails and his position as a heavenly god declined. By the Middle Babylonian period, writes Katz, he was considered as Ereshkigal's spouse, even though the elevation to that status may already have begun in the late Old Babylonian period.[18]

Certain links of Scorpio with the netherworld can be seen in tablet IX of the Standard Babylonian version of *The Epic of Gilgamesh*. Gilgamesh reached the entrance of the netherworld and found that the guards were two scorpion-beings[19]:

> There were scorpion-men guarding its gate,
> Whose terror was dread, whose glance was death,
> Whose radiance was fearful, overwhelming the mountains,
> At sunrise and sunset they guarded the sun. (IX 42-45; George 1999).

In the *Epic of Gilgamesh*, the scorpion-man guarding the entrance of the netherworld is spelled in Akkadian *girtablullû*, which is a composition of the words *gír-tab* (scorpion) and lú-ùllu (untamed man).[20] F. A. M. Wiggerman writes that a couple of *girtablullû*, a scorpion man and a scorpion woman, guard the gate of mount *Māšu*, which is the entrance of the Netherworld, and watch over the rising and the setting of the Sun. The Akkadian word *Māšu* means "Twin."[21] The entrance of the Netherworld consisted of two twin mountains. The word *kur* in Sumerian means both mountain and netherworld.[22] In another context, the gods *Lugal-irra* and *Meslamta-ea* were thought to stand at the entrance to the Netherworld ready to dismember the dead as they entered.

Astronomical texts also explain the constellation of Gemini as *Lugal-irra* and *Meslamta-ea*.[23] Accordinng to Roberts, the god *Erra* associated to Nergal was sometimes spelled "*Irra.*"[24]

In addition, *Nergal* not only added the features of the warrior god *Erra*, but by the Old Babylonian period, *Nergal* assimilated several rival Sumerian chthonic gods such as *Ninazu*, and *Meslamta-ea*.[25] In the Old Babylonian period the cult of *Nergal* is attested in Nippur, Ur, Uruk, Sippar, Dilbat and Isin.[26]

In order to add further evidence that *Nergal* was a netherworld deity, in the Neo-Assyrian literature poem known as *the Underworld Vision of an Assyrian Prince*, a prince who might be Ashurbanipal, comes face to face with the netherworld god *Nergal*, and sees the god as a luminescent being.[27]

Nergal as a Hero

In the wider context of Sumerian mythology *Nergal* was regarded as hero and son of Enlil in Nippur. *Ninurta* was also a hero-god son of Enlil. The *Anzu myth* tells how *Ninurta* retrieved the tablet of destinies and killed Anzu, the evil bird who stole the tablet from Enlil. According to A. Livingstone, in the old Babylonian period *Nergal* took on the epithet of "avenger of his father Enlil" and shared such epithet with the hero *Ninurta* who, along with *Zababa*, could be identified with *Nergal*.[28]

According to Jeremy Black and Anthony Green, during the Parthian period the god Nergal was equated to the Greek Heracles.[29] One of the first labors of Heracles was to kill the Nemean lion. Even though there might have been lions in Greece, according to Black, lions were very common in Mesopotamia until the end of the third millennium BCE, and it seems that the last lion in Mesopotamia was killed in twentieth century CE! In the Epic of Gilgamesh, the gods discuss whether to send a plague of lions instead of the flood would a more appropriate chastisement.[30] Heracles is usually depicted wearing the skin of a lion, a theme which more in tune with Mesopotamia or with the Near East than with Greece.

The lion-demon or *ugallu*, depicted in the Neo-Assyrian palace reliefs, was a beneficent demon protective against evil demons and illnesses. On Old-Babylonian seals, however, he often holds a man upside down from one leg and is associated with Nergal, or with his attendant, and is considered a bringer of disease.

The figure of the lion is certainly associated with Nergal, which later on was associated in certain places with Heracles. Nergal was indeed considered a hero since his inception in Mesopotamia as a brother of Ninurta, another hero-god.

Conclusion

The combative attributes of the Babylonian *Nergal* are deeply embedded in Mars and our Western culture displays it in words such as "martial arts." Even though there is not explicitly attested in cuneiform tablets that *Nergal* was the ruler of Aries and Scorpio, the attributes of war, fight, and the heroic side of Nergal are attributes of Mars as ruler of Aries, whereas *Nergal* as an underworld deity associated to death, plagues, and the underworld are characteristics of Mars as ruler of the Scorpio.

The conclusion is that the attributes assigned to the Babylonian god *Nergal* have so many things in common with the Greek god Ares and the Roman god Mars that both Mars and Ares seem to derive from *Nergal*, which in Babylon was associated to the planet Mars.

Endnotes

[1] Ptolemy, *Tetrabiblos*, ed. and translated by F. E. Robbins (Cambridge: Harvard University Press, 1971 [1940]), p. 81.
[2] Ulla Koch-Westenholz, *Mesopotamian Astrology: An Introduction to Babylonian and Assyrian Celestial Divination* (Copenhagen: Museum Tusculanum Press, 1995), p. 128.

³Koch-Westenholz, *Mesopotamian Astrology*, p. 128.
⁴Leick, Gwendolyn, *A Dictionary of Ancient Near Eastern Mythology* (London: Routlegde, 1991), p.127.
⁵J.J.M. Roberts, *The Earliest Semitic Pantheon: A Study of the Semitic Deities Attested in Mesopotamia before Ur III* (Baltimore: The John Hopkins University Press, 1972), p.150.
⁶Black, *Gods, Demons and Symbols of Ancient Mesopotamia*, p. 135.
⁷Thorkild Jacobsen, *The Treasures of Darkness: A History of Mesopotamian Religion* (New Haven: Yale University Press, 1976), p. 227.
⁸Jeremy Black and Anthony Green, *Gods, Demons and Symbols of Ancient Mesopotamia* (London: British Museum Press, 1998 [1992]), p. 136.
⁹Black, *Gods, Demons and Symbols of Ancient Mesopotamia*, p. 136.
¹⁰Jeremy Black and Anthony Green, *Gods, Demons and Symbols of Ancient Mesopotamia* (London: British Museum Press, 1998 [1992]).
¹¹Leick, Gwendolyn, *A Dictionary of Ancient Near Eastern Mythology* (London: Routlegde, 1991), p.127.
¹²Dina Katz, *The Image of the Netherworld in the Sumerian sources* (Bethesda: CDL Press, 2003), p. 363.
¹³Leick, *A Dictionary of Ancient Near Eastern Mythology*, p.128.
¹⁴Katz, *The Image of the Netherworld in the Sumerian sources*, p. 360.
¹⁵Leick, *A Dictionary of Ancient Near Eastern Mythology*, p. 47.
¹⁶Samuel Noah Kramer, *Sumerian Mythology: A Study of Spiritual and Literary Achievement in the Third Millenium B.C.* (Philadelphia: University of Pennsylvania Press, 1972 [1944]), p. 43.
¹⁷Stephanie Dalley, *Myths from Mesopotamia: Creation, The Flood, Gilgamesh, and Others* (Oxford: Oxford University Press, 2008 [1991]), p. 163.
¹⁸Katz, *The Image of the Netherworld in the Sumerian sources*, p. 363.
¹⁹M. A. Ataç, "The Melammu aas Divine Epiphany and Usurped Entity," *Ancient Near Eastern Art in Context: Studies in Honor of Irene J. Winter by Her Studies*, ed. by Jack Cheng and Marian H. Feldman (Leiden: Brill, 2007), p. 299.

[20]F. A. M. Wiggerman, *Mesopotamian Protective Spirits: The Ritual Texts* (Groningen: Styx Publications, 1992), p. 180.
[21]Wiggerman, *Mesopotamian Protective Spirits*, p. 180.
22Kramer, *Sumerian Mythology*, p. 76.
[23]Mehmet-Ali Ataç "The 'Underworld Vision' of the Ninevite Intellectual Milieu," Iraq, Vol. 66, *Nineveh. Papers of the 49th Rencontre Assyriologique Internationale*, Part One (2004), p. 72.
[24]J. J. M. Roberts, *The Earliest Semitic Pantheon: A Study of the Semitic Deities Attested in Mesopotamia before Ur III* (Baltimore: The John Hopkins University Press, 1972), p. 22.
[25]Leick, *A Dictionary of Ancient Near Eastern Mythology*, pp.127-8
[26]Livingstone, *Dictionary of Deities and Demons in the Bible*, p. 622.
[27]Ataç, Mehmet-Ali, "The Melammu as Divine Epiphany and Usurped Entity," Ancient Near Eastern Art in Context: Studies in Honor of Irene J. Winter by Her Studies, ed. by Jack Cheng and Marian H. Feldman (Leiden: Brill, 2007), p. 299-300.
[28]A. Livingstone, ed. by K. van Der Toorn, B. Becking and P. W. Van Der Horst, *Dictionary of Deities and Demons in the Bible* (Leiden: Brill, 1999), p. 622.
[29]Black, *Gods, Demons and Symbols of Ancient Mesopotamia*, p. 136.
[30]Black, *Gods, Demons and Symbols of Ancient Mesopotamia*, p. 118.

Bibliography

Ataç, Mehmet-Ali, "The 'Underworld Vision' of the Ninevite Intellectual Milieu," *Nineveh. Papers of the 49th Rencontre Assyriologique Internationale, Part One*. Iraq, vol. 66, (2004), pp. 67-76.

Ataç, Mehmet-Ali, "The Melammu as Divine Epiphany and Usurped Entity," Ancient Near Eastern Art in Context: Studies in Honor of Irene J. Winter by Her Studies, ed. by Jack Cheng and Marian H. Feldman (Leiden: Brill, 2007).

Black, Jeremy, and Green, Anthony, *Gods, Demons and Symbols of Ancient Mesopotamia* (London: British Museum Press, 1998 [1992]).

Dalley, Stephanie, *Myths from Mesopotamia: Creation, The Flood, Gilgamesh, and Others* (Oxford: Oxford University Press, 2008

[1991]).
Jacobsen, Thorkild, *The Treasures of Darkness: A History of Mesopotamian Religion* (New Haven: Yale University Press, 1976).
Katz, Dina, *The Image of the Netherworld in the Sumerian sources* (Bethesda: CDL Press, 2003).
Koch-Westenholz, Ulla, *Mesopotamian Astrology: An Introduction to Babylonian and Assyrian Celestial Divination* (Copenhagen: Museum Tusculanum Press, 1995).
Kramer, Samuel Noah, *Sumerian Mythology: A Study of Spiritual and Literary Achievement in the Third Millenium B.C.* (Philadelphia: University of Pennsylvania Press, 1972 [1944]).
Lambert, W. G., 'Studies in Nergal', *Bibliotheca Orientalis 30*, 1973, pp. 355-63.
Leick, Gwendolyn, *A Dictionary of Ancient Near Eastern Mythology* (London: Routlegde, 1991).
Ptolemy, *Tetrabiblos*, ed. and translated by Robbins, F. E. (Cambridge: Harvard University Press, 1971 [1940]).
Roberts, J. J. M., *The Earliest Semitic Pantheon: A Study of the Semitic Deities Attested in Mesopotamia before Ur III* (Baltimore: The John Hopkins University Press, 1972).
Van Der Toorn, K., Becking, B., and Van Der Horst, P. W. (eds.), *Dictionary of Deities and Demons in the Bible* (Leiden: Brill, 1999).
Wiggerman, F. A. M., *Mesopotamian Protective Spirits: The Ritual Texts* (Groningen: Styx Publications, 1992).

Esoteric Jewish Astrology

By Karni Zor

ABSTRACT: Although the practice of astrology is forbidden in some Jewish orthodox sects, astrology throughout the millennia was well embedded in the Jewish tradition. Astrology is mentioned in the Jewish texts in different traditional interpretations of the bible and in the esoteric practice of the Kabala. Actually, the Old Testament offers some fascinating exoteric knowledge to do with astrology. This article offers a glimpse at the ways the art of astrology was traditionally referred to, mentioned, and practiced in Judaism for thousands of years.

Introduction

Being an astrologer in Israel can be a bit awkward at times. Although Israel is a very modern country, in which new-age activities and spiritual treatments and consultations are abundant, astrology has a special problem. And that is that in the eyes of most orthodox Jews astrology is actually strictly forbidden. Therefore, orthodox Jews will not come to an astrologer for consultation. But because many of the people in Israel, who are not orthodox themselves, will have an orthodox background or orthodox family members, from time to time I will hear the question, almost whispered in my ear: "But, isn't IT forbidden?"

Then I will usually go into a lengthy explanation that serves to calm that person, allowing him or her to accept the astrological advice they so want to receive. I will explain to them that not only is astrology not forbidden but it is even mentioned in the Bible in numerous ways, and has been practiced by Jews throughout the millennia.

This article offers a glimpse at the ways the art of astrology was traditionally referred to, mentioned and practiced in Judaism for thousands of years. I think that any fan of astrology will find fascinating the esoteric astrological knowledge found in a text written more than 3,000 years ago.

The Astrological Debate in Judaism

At the end of the 5th century there was a huge debate between Jewish leaders about whether to refer to astrology. Some of the Jewish leaders and rabbis not only accepted astrology as a tool of guidance but even practiced astrology themselves, writing about the different characters of the astrological signs and the influence of the planets upon people's lives. Others referred to astrology as the practice of pagans, strictly condemning the use of it in the monotheistic tradition.[1]

Since then the two voices have been heard in the Jewish courts. We can see Jewish scholars like Rabbi Yom Tov Ben Abraham Shvili (born around 1300 BC) writing that ". . . a person born under the Sun's influence will achieve leadership and greatness whilst that who was born under the influence of the Moon will suffer great difficulties,"[2] while other scholars like Rabbi Moshe Ben Mimon (born 1138 BC) writes that astrology is considered paganism and has no influence upon a person's life.[3]

But since Judaism goes back well before the 5th century, one can actually see that before that millennia when this debate started, astrology was well embedded in the Jewish tradition. Astrology is mentioned in the Old Testament in different traditional interpretations of the Bible and in the esoteric practice of the Kabala.

A Glimpse to a Lost History

I have to confess that being a non-practicing Jew and having my master's degree in comparative religions I do not take the stories of the Old Testament as absolute truths. Nevertheless, even if we do not relate to the stories of the Old Testament as historical truths, they do allow us a glimpse into early cultures, just as do texts written more than 3,000 years ago. The biblical stories tell us something about ancient times and forgotten history.

According to the Old Testament the first Jew, Abraham, was told by God to leave his homeland and move to a new land, the land of Israel. Abraham's old home was in Horan, a city in Mesopotamia. And Mesopotamia is, among other things, the birth place of astrology. Ancient archaeological relics show us that astrology and astronomy were practiced in Mesopotamia as early as 3000 BC[4]—that is, 5,000 years ago.

Among the artifacts found in Mesopotamia one can find drawings of astrological wheels and ephemerides that follow the movement the planets.[5] It is known that later on, in Babylonia (the kingdom that rose in Mesopotamia around 2000 BC) the astrologers held a special place and rulers often consulted with them often.[6]

As all travelers of his time, Abraham must have used the stars for navigating towards the unknown country he was heading to. But Abraham did not use the stars solely for navigation. One of the first things he was told by the Lord, according to the Old Testament, was to look up at the skies for his own destiny: "I will multiply thy seed as the stars of the heaven."[7] The legends say that Abraham knew the language of the stars and that he was one of the Mesopotamian magi. So when Abraham left his old country he probably took the knowledge of the stars with him, passing on the astrological knowledge outside of Mesopotamia and further to the west.

The Israelites' connection to the stars continued with Joseph, one of Abraham's successors who needed to move on from the Promised Land and relocate to the nearby land of Egypt. Egypt, as we know, was another ancient culture that held much knowledge of the stars, their movements and their application upon human life (we will not go here to Egyptian astrology, which is another fascinating theme in itself). In the biblical story, Joseph carried on the family tradition of astrology and found himself the Pharaoh's personal advisor, telling him of forcoming events.[8]

Before going to Egypt, young Joseph had a dream. In his dream 11 stars, the Moon, and the Sun bowed before Joseph. Later his dream became a reality, when Joseph's 11 brothers, together with his mother and father, came to meet him in Egypt, not knowing this was their lost brother and son, and bowing before him as he was the pharaoh's great consultant.[9] I think it is quite amazing to see that in a text written more than 3,000 years ago, the Sun and Moon are referred to as symbols of the father and the mother, astrological knowledge that we as astrologers almost take for granted, but here we can see the very early roots of this.

Joseph and his 11 brothers, the 12 sons of Israel, were the establishing fathers of the 12 tribes of Israel, which are tightly connected to the 12 astrological signs.

Esoteric Knowledge of Astrology in the Book of Genesis

The Jewish esoteric study of the Kabala relates to the stories in the Old Testament not as actual events but rather as clues for universal knowledge. And universal knowledge, especially related to astrology, can definitely be found in the book of *Genesis* in the way the Kabala interprets them.

In the story that unfolds in the first book of the Old Testament, *Genesis*, we find some interesting references that will catch the attention of the astrology fan. The biblical stories tell about the three fathers of the nation: Abraham, Isaac, and Jacob. They also tell about four great mothers: Sarah, Rebecca, Rachel, and Leah. Together, these seven ancestors parented 12 sons, later to become the 12 tribes of Israel.

Threefold and fourfold patterns, together with numbers like seven, and definitely the mentioning of a dozen brothers, are the sort of thing that gladdens the hearts of astrology lovers. When we think of it, the fundamentals of astrology are the 12 signs (or houses) founded from the different combinations of the four elements (earth, water, air, and fire) and three modalities (fixed, cardinal, and mutable), governed by the seven classical rulers (Sun, Moon, Mercury, Venus, Mars, Jupiter and Saturn).

A further look will actually reveal that the three fathers of the Jewish nation held three different personalities that acutely correlate to the three modes—fixed, mutable, and cardinal. Abraham, the founder of the nation, followed the words of the lord without tilting left or right, showing a fixed character. Isaac was of a good temper. Even his name tells of his pleasant character, as it means literally "he shall laugh" in Hebrew. Therefore, Isaac can correspond to the mutable mode. And Jacob was a troublemaker. While in his mother's womb he was already opposed to his twin brother. Later on Jacob tricked Esau into giving him the right to inherit from their father. When Jacob later fought an angel and defeated it, he was renamed Israel, which means "the one who confronted god himself and defeated him"; this shows the traits that represent the cardinal mode.[10]

By the way, the name Abraham contains a puzzle; it is an anagram for "Brahma." Brahma was the creator god in the Hindu (or Brahmin) tradition that rose about the same time as Judaism. Brahma worked as part of a triad of three gods that held the cosmic principle of positive, negative and neutral. Brahma was the creator (positive—cardinal), Vishnu the preserver (neutral—fixed), and Shiva the destroyer (minus—mutable).[11]

The Wondrous 12

The *Book of Numbers* in the Old Testament seems to deal a lot with the number of people in each one of the 12 tribes and gives in-depth details about the whereabouts and location of each tribe during the Israelites' 40-year journey in the desert. According to the Kabala, the number of people mentioned in each tribe does not represent an actual count of people but rather depicts the number of stars in each constellation of the zodiac associated with each tribe. The location of each tribe in the camp represents esoteric knowledge that has much to do with astrology.

In Jacob's blessing to his 12 sons, Jacob describes Dan (Scorpio) as a snake biting the horse rider's leg. The snake of course, is the symbol of Scorpio, and the rider is Sagittarius. And in fact the part of Scorpio's constellation that "invades" the realm of Sagittarius is also known as Ophiuchus, The Snake-Bearer. Further on Jacob depicts Judea as a lion (Leo) and Ephraim as a bull.[12]

According to the Kabala each one of the 12 tribes of Israel is associated with a constellation of the zodiac:

Aries, Gad	Taurus, Ephraim
Gemini, Menashe	Cancer, Issachar
Leo, Judea	Virgo, Naphtali
Libra, Asher	Scorpio, Dan
Sagittarius, Binyamin	Capricorn, Zvulon
Aquarius, Reuven	Pisces, Shimon

Each tribe is also associated with a gemstone that could be found on the great priest's breastplate.[13] This article does not go into the depth of gemstones and astrology, but those who know about the qualities of the gemstones can see that each tribe was given the gemstone that would counterbalance its natural tendencies (for example, relaxing amethyst was given to Aries, focusing agate to Sagittarius and so on.

Following the Clues and My Own Investigation

The Bible is filled with riddles, clues, and hints of the esoteric meaning behind the 12 tribes.

One of these clues is presented in the description of the locations of the 12 Israelite tribes around the Tabernacle during their voyage in the desert to the Holy Land.[14] This is how the tribes camped each night, three tribes on each of the Tabernacle's directions:

East—Camp of Judah, which included the tribes Judah, Issachar and Zebulun

South—Camp of Reuben; Reuben, Simeon and Gad

West—Camp of Ephraim; Ephraim, Mannasseh and Benjamin

North—Camp of Dan; Dan, Asher and Naphtali

When I followed the clues left to us by the biblical authors I found myself uncovering ancient tradition and knowledge, just like a detective, and revealing some fascinating finds. The following is part of my research investigating the astrological clues presented in the text of old testaments.

The biblical division of the twelve tribes to four sets of three caught my attention immediately. As astrologers we are used to seeing the table of elements and modalities, so finding this kind of set-up hinted that something astrological might be hiding here.

My interest grew as I realized that the leaders of each camp were the tribes associated with the four cardinal signs: Leo (Judah), Aquarius (Reuben), Taurus (Ephraim) and Scorpio

(Dan). I then thought I might find the other two tribes of each camp as representatives of the other two modalities. But this was not the case. Putting aside the disappointment, I saw something even more fascinating than having the actual table of elements and modalities in the tribe's layout, something that I most definitely did not expect to find.

Let's take a second look at the position of the tribes in the camp:

East—Leo, Cancer and Capricorn

South—Aquarius, Pisces and Aries

North—Taurus, Gemini and Sagittarius

West—Scorpio, Libra and Virgo

What are these combinations trying to tell us? Aquarius, Pisces, and Aries are obviously following signs. So are Scorpio, Libra and Virgo, but in backward order. But the other two sets are quite strange at first glance.

Looking again, something fascinating is revealed: Leo is assigned to Cancer, which is the sign preceding it, and to Capricorn. The line of Capricorn and Cancer mark Earth's tilt between the tropic of Capricorn and the tropic of Cancer. Taurus is associated with its following sign, Gemini, and to Sagittarius. The line between Sagittarius and Gemini is a very important line astronomically as it marks the region of the sky in which our Milky Way galaxy can be seen at night.

But could the ancients once have known about Earth's tilt between the tropic of Cancer and Capricorn and the astronomical whereabouts of our Milky Way? We do need to remember that the Bible is at least 3,000 years old. The answer to the question remains unknown. But what we can tell is that three millennia ago the knowledge of astrology was abundant and rich in the land set between Mesopotamia and Egypt.

Epilogue

As it is hard to overcome years of tradition and deep psychologies I cannot yet say that I have managed to convince many orthodox Jews to refer to astrology. But what I do know is that although not commonly accepted today in the eyes of the Jewish believers, astrology was definitely practiced in the land of Israel and throughout the ages and that much esoteric astrological knowledge is embedded in the original Jewish most sacred text, the Old Testament itself.

Endnotes

[1] *Talmud Bavli, Masechet Shabat*, p. 156.
[2] Ibid.
[3] Rabbi Moshe Ben Mimon. *Igeret Taiman*, chapters 3, 4 and 7.
[4] Tester, S. Jim. *A History of Western Astrology*. Woodbridge, Suffolk: Boydell Press, 1987.
[5] Rochberg, Francesa, 1998. *Babylonian Horoscopes*. American Philosophical Society.
[6] Baigent, Michael, 1994. *From the Omens of Babylon: Astrology and Ancient Mesopotamia*. Arkana.
[7] Holden, James Herschel, 1996. *A History of Horoscopic Astrology*. AFA.
[8] Koch-Westenholz, Ulla, 1995. *Mesopotamian Astrology*, volume 19 of CNI publications. Museum Tusculanum Press.
[9] *Genesis* 22, 17.
[10] *Genesis*, 39, 40, 41.
[11] *Bhagavad Gita*, 4: 8.
[12] *Genesis*, 37.
[13] Zohar interpretation of *Genesis*.
[14] *Book of Numbers*, 2.

Astrology of the Sequester

Obama's 20-hour Standoff and the Difference It Made

By Sylvia Sky

ABSTRACT: The infamous sequester mandating automatic and across-the-board U.S. federal budget cuts was to go into effect on Friday, March 1, 2013—but when? Its supporters in Congress said it went into effect at midnight. President Obama said it would not go into effect until he signed the order. Inviting further negotiations on a punishing and poorly designed plan, Obama waited all day, until 8:30 p.m. His wait created a media event that served to ennoble him, take the teeth out of the order and the wind from the sails of his mostly Republican opponents. Set up to persist for ten years, the sequester would have a much shorter and ineffective life. Horoscope charts for March 1, 2013 at midnight and at 8:30 p.m. are compared and analyzed.

A U.S. law passed in 2011 required 10 years of cuts in federal spending starting on March 1, 2013. Supporters of this budget-balancing plan said it took effect at midnight on March 1. But President Barack Obama, who favored a less drastic plan, declared that the cuts, collectively called "the seques-

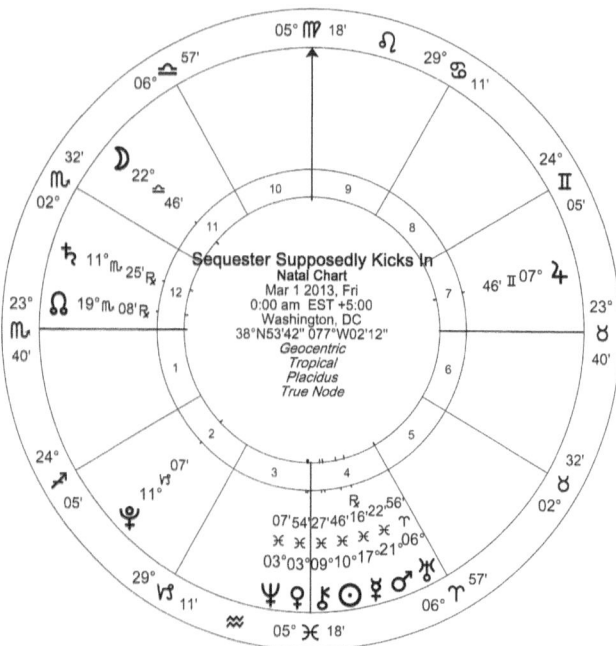

ter," would start on March 1 only after he signed the order.

The sequester was a counterweight to a federal budget with trillions of dollars in expenses and deficits. It was designed to save $1.2 trillion dollars over 10 years through automatic cuts to and caps on federal programs. These included defense programs, national security, NASA, the National Institutes of Health, federal food assistance, and Head Start.

Developed by a Congress deeply divided along party lines, the sequester was a compromise neither party liked. No one knew what its effects might be. Further negotiations were expected but did not occur. On January 2, Obama signed a law postponing the sequester until March 1. All day on Friday, March 1, he held off on signing the order, which the public by then distrusted and feared. It was supposed to have kicked in on March 1, 2013, at midnight.

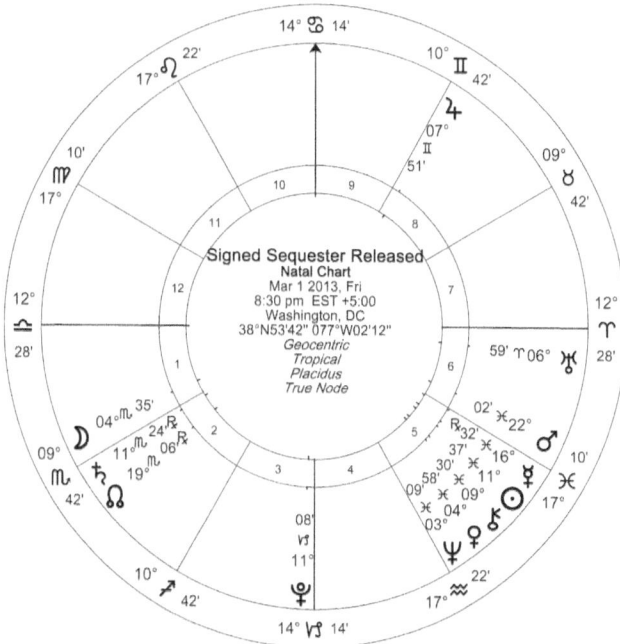

The media had set the public's nerves on edge by broadcasting chilling speculations about the sequester's possible effects: weakened national security, layoffs in defense-related industries, hungry children, and unpaid furloughs for federal workers.

Obama hoped for further negotiations and when they did not happen the White House publicly released the signed order on March 1 at 8:30 p.m. EST. The second chart shown here was cast for 8:30 p.m., 20 hours and 30 minutes after midnight. The wait made a difference not in the law but how the public received it.

The sequester's inception was an event. But if the 12:00 a.m. sequester were for a person, he or she would have a:

- Pisces Sun in the fourth house
- Libra Moon in the eleventh house

- Scorpio Ascendant
- Virgo Midheaven

This "person," while appearing compassionate and accommodating (Pisces Sun, Libra Moon), does intricate work in groups (Moon in the eleventh house) and behind the scenes (Scorpio Ascendant). The person's Libra Moon indicates that balance and justice are his or her deepest desires. The fault is in believing that like a father or patriarch (stellium in the fourth house), he or she can settle domestic issues with acts of will. This person's mainspring (Sun in the fourth house) is in fact home, property, and family. The career (Virgo Midheaven) is one of service and frugality. The sequester was one of many austerity measures Congress called for in its Budget Control Act of 2011.

If the 8:30 p.m. sequester chart were for a person, he or she would have a:

- Pisces Sun in the fifth house
- Scorpio Moon in the first house
- Libra Ascendant
- Cancer Midheaven

Again, a Pisces Sun is basically compassionate, but with a Scorpio Moon it is also passionate, plus stubborn to a fault. Aware that his Scorpio Moon stubbornness and wariness compensate for a desire to be loved, with Libra rising the person makes conscious efforts to appear reasonable and fair. Even so, with the Scorpio Moon in the first house, at times the person acts impulsively or vengefully. The Cancer midheaven shows that his or her career goals are care and unity. Uniting a divided governing body and nation is hard work, but with the Sun in the fifth house he or she believes it might be creatively accomplished.

The midnight chart sounds like the Republican leadership

that put its collective foot down and said the sequester started March 1 at midnight. The 8:30 p.m. chart seems more like the Democrats, represented by President Obama, who along with his party proposed tax changes to offset the cuts in domestic programs.

On March 1, Obama played his last card—declaring himself in charge, and waiting until 8:30 p.m. to publicly admit defeat.

What the Waiting Accomplished

Obama's stalling on March 1 demonstrated hope for compromise and his party's concern about the cuts to social programs. In photographs he appeared patient, pained, and compassionate. The 20-hour wait stole the spotlight from sequester backers, redirecting the day's attention toward the president.

His defeat was bitter. On March 5, the White House announced that because of sequester budget cuts it was closing its doors to public tours starting March 9. This was widely criticized as an unnecessary and vindictive move and a public relations error. White House tours resumed on November 5, 2013.

Later decisions and negotiations softened some of the sequester's harsher or more unpopular effects, such as cuts to veterans' benefits.

8:30 p.m. and the U.S. Birth Chart

The 8:30 p.m. sequester chart has three advantages that would mitigate the sudden budget cuts and leave the door open to negotiations, which the midnight chart doesn't do.

In the 8:30 p.m. chart the Sun, Moon and Midheaven (in Pisces, Scorpio, and Cancer) harmonize; they are all in water signs that go with the flow.

The 8:30 p.m. chart might better please and benefit the American citizenry because of the Sun's trine aspect to the Moon. Both charts have the Sun in Pisces, yet only the 8:30 p.m.

chart has the Sun, representing power and authority, firmly favoring the Moon, representing the masses. By contrast, at midnight March 1, the Moon was in Libra in the eleventh house, a sesquiquadrate to Mars its only aspect. At that hour the public felt acted upon rather than part of the lawmaking process.

The midnight chart tucks the masses away in the eleventh house of organizations and groups, where they are the masses with only a biquintile "Get 'er done" link to the Sun. At 8:30 p.m. the Moon, now in Scorpio, occupied the first house. With that, the sequester's effect on the public took priority.

We must note in the 8:30 p.m. chart the position of its Midheaven at 14 Cancer. The U.S. Sibly chart has its natal Sun at 13 Cancer. This conjunction is favorable. Our chief executive, although forced to concede, looked not like a loser but like a victor and defender of democracy. There is also a chance that the sequester might eventually be called a first (wobbly) step toward a balanced and healthy federal budget.

Where These Charts Are Alike

A chart set for any hour on March 1, 2013, will show five planets plus the asteroid Chiron in a very unusual cluster. Neptune, Venus, Chiron, the Sun, Mercury (retrograde), and Mars were wedged in a narrow 18-degree span, like pellets packed into a shotgun shell. In both charts the many empty houses signify that the U.S. was left vulnerable on other fronts while the self-made "fiscal cliff" domestic budget crisis played out.

In this crowded 18-degree span, five planets and Chiron were in Pisces, emphasizing this most spiritual and other-worldly zodiac sign. Astrologically, the tangled roots of the sequester compromise are vanity (Venus), daydreams (Neptune conjunction Venus), short-term thinking (Mercury), ego (Sun), favoritism (Venus conjunction Sun) and wars (Mars).

The Pisces Sun was conjunct retrograde Mercury retrograde

and in its detriment, and Mercury and Mars were conjunct: conditions encouraging faulty decision-making.

The Pisces stellium also shows a crisis of faith. Few citizens can have faith in a government so expensive and deeply in debt that the numbers are almost incomprehensible. In both charts the asteroid Chiron conjunction the Sun exposes the nation's weakness so that healing might begin. The sequester law was strong medicine. Yet both charts show that it was not necessarily the best medicine.

Creative Disinformation and "Nobody Knows"

The friction between political parties and reluctance to compromise are represented in both charts by the long-lasting Uranus-Pluto square. In the midnight sequester chart Pluto is in the house of money and values, showing the sequester initiative as part of an agonizingly slow but necessary change in the country's wealth management and what its people value.

In the 8:30 chart, Pluto in the third house of communications is square Uranus in the sixth house of work and service. The media, in flux while evolving new forms of communication (represented by Pluto), told citizens about the government's fiscal crisis and that the sequester might threaten the small gains made in the nation's economy and job market since the crash of 2008. An exasperating Uranus in the sixth house meant that the jobs we had didn't feel secure.

Partly because of its self-involved Scorpio Moon in the first house and the stellium in the fifth house, the 8:30 p.m. chart's creative potential became creative disinformation, worry, and blame, and when the news came out, the Moon-Saturn conjunction made it sound to the public like another cross to bear.

By waiting until 8:30 when the Moon was trine the Venus-Neptune conjunction, Obama's 20-hour standoff looked not like stubbornness but like righteous resistance. Although the standoff didn't work and it might have been a media ploy, the same was true of the sequester itself.

The media labeled the sequester "a political football" with each party using it for self-serving reasons. President Obama said it was Congress' idea; Congress said the idea was Obama's. Few knew exactly what the sequester was. Confident sequester backer and Republican House Speaker John Boehner admitted on television's *Meet the Press*: "I don't know whether it's going to hurt the economy or not. I don't think anyone quite understands how the sequester is really going to work."

In both sequester charts, Jupiter, in its detriment in Gemini, is square and afflicts the stellium, which doesn't need more affliction. Saturn in Scorpio is trine the stellium, saying the time was truly ripe for facing and correcting the nation's fiscal mess.

The law, on paper, was the same whether it took effect at midnight or 8:30 p.m. But at 8:30 p.m. the public felt more satisfied that compromise had been invited if not made. No one disagreed, then or now, that the U.S. government must stop bleeding money. Yet the charts with the Sun, a retrograde Mercury, Venus, Neptune, and Chiron all piled up in Pisces should have told us that the sequester as enacted, no matter at what hour, was a fantasy remedy.

The sequester has since been largely superseded by the Bipartisan Budget Act of 2015, which gave President Obama more of what he and his party wanted. It was not a factor in the president's budget for fiscal 2016. Again, he had waited for the right moment, and at that time the moment was right.

Qualitative Research
Narrative Report on the Personal Lunar Cycle

By Aureal Williams

ABSTRACT: This qualitative research narrative reviews 21 years' experience working with rhythm of the Personal Lunar Cycle, from the "recovering" of the technique through a kinesthetic body experience, to tracking it for two years, to writing about it, teaching it, and documenting it in blog posts. The working hypothesis of this research suggests that, like the Collective Lunar Cycle from one New Moon to the next, The Personal Lunar Cycle, based on the Sun-Moon phase angle at birth, offers a pattern of energy that is reliably predictable. Benefits of planning and scheduling with the Personal Lunar Cycle include increased synchronicity and decreased stress related to a strengthened sense of connection with the cosmos. Broader research on this technique is warranted.

Genesis

In 1995, through a kinesthetic body experience, I "recovered" a technique that I have named the Personal Lunar Cycle. This recovering of a technique came through a relaxation experience. I left a position as clinical research nurse coordinator on National Institutes of Health HIV research project at a time when HIV research was highly completive; people were dying of AIDS and scientists rushed to find a cure.

The work stress overwhelmed me and I decided to leave that position and go out on my own as a relaxation expert. One afternoon, a couple of months after leaving that position, I stretched out on my bed wondering, begging, pleading, really, about why I was so tired. I no longer had an unpredictable commute with a boss who demanded I be on time; I no longer had the day-to-day stress of young mothers and their children dying from AIDS; I no longer had the exposure of cut-throat stress in a scientific, competitive, clinical environment. I was relaxed, living in a bucolic setting, working on relaxation training and could not understand why I was so tired.

I had my calendar next to me as I rested on the bed. I used the American Federation of Astrologers calendar that was still being published at the time. (This calendar is available through Matrix Day Watch software and continues to be my preferred astrological calendar because it gives the Sun-Moon phase angle in the lower right block of each day's section on the calendar.)

In a synchronous moment I noticed that the Sun-Moon phase angle at that time was just before the Sun-Moon phase angle of my birth. I was in a Dark Moon phase in a personal lunar cycle! The discovery that my energy level could be equated with my lunar birth phase was an astounding realization.

Since the late 1960s I had been aware of the Dark Moon as an energetic pull to stillness. Based on decades of personal experience, I consider the Dark Moon as a reliable predictive of energy levels. In addition, it is on Dark Moon days when out shopping, I overhear other shoppers say to one another, "I am so tired and I don't know why." I know why: the Dark Moon is a naturally occurring low energy time and our bodies have resonance with this rhythm.

To wake to the experience that there is a personal cycle of energy along with the collective cycle of energy based on lunar phases was a life-changing event, rooting me into a deeper experience of the lunar-human connection.

Cycles, the Nature of Life

Life is cyclic by nature. This, we know; however, do we consciously live it? My Soul longs for the time when community lived by Moon Flow. There was a building phase to activity and a dissolving phase. My body feels this rhythm.

I can remember in 1979, in acute distress, pleading with my therapist, "Half the month I have energy and the other half I do not." Even though I was actively working with astrology at the time, it was not in my consciousness that this is the nature of life, this ebb and this flow mirrored for us each month in the Moon's flow. Some of us feel this natural cycling more viscerally than others. I am one who feels it and my life has been a path of understanding and teaching this awareness.

While astrology is based on a study of cycles, we can also look to metaphysical traditions to appreciate our blood bond with cyclic living. From *Cycles in Nature and the Fate of the Human Soul*, no author identified,[1] we read, "In Nature, the Great Cycle is divided into two: the semicircle of activity called Manvantara, and the other half-circle of rest called Pralaya. This is the basic principle of the Law of Cycles—activity and rest." This is the Moon's flow, building Moon and dissolving Moon, and the foundation for understanding the receiving and release pattern of cyclic living.

If something is in our blood and bones to live and teach and share, we do it; this is a path many astrologers have chosen. For me, the path is about the inherent alignment of cycles in nature with physical energy. There is no separation; we are cosmic beings and living the cyclic pattern represents our evolutionary path.

As Armin Zebrowski writes in *Cycles: The Eternal Impulse of Nature*[2], the transition when one cycle ends and before the next begins is critical. This is the zero stillpoint where conscious transcendence of duality is possible.

While cycles rule our world, their illusion of duality—building/dissolving; light/dark, good/bad is a trap, because cycles, by their very essence, are whole. From ancient religions to modern culture, though, the trap of duality is in our consciousness.

Again, from *Cycles: The Eternal Impulse of Nature*, Zebrowski writes that in transcending duality, "The necessary pattern for life, consciousness, recognition, and evolution comes forth. We constantly experience such transitions—but not consciously.[3]

Experiencing this transition consciously is, to me, a call for now. Working with the Personal Lunar Cycle, I have had visceral, sensate, conscious experience of this zero point, an infinity within stillness, as one Personal Lunar Cycle rhythm ends and the next begins. This exquisite pivot point is deep, profound, exquisite and real. Opening to this experience comes though awareness of physical energy levels with cyclic flow and our Moon is a sacred, loving teacher.

Another feature of cycles is their spiraling nature. As Scott J. Osterhage writes in *Inherent Rhythms of Life*[4], a spiraling nature of cycles differentiates the revolution/evolution experience of cycles. In astrology, we appreciate this evolutionary nature of cycles through the recognition that one cycle builds on the next. The inheritance within cycles is seen through a study of Saros cycles, for instance, and Dietrech Pessin's great work on lunar families[5].

Astrology's beloved teacher, Rudyar, writes: "The study of cycles—that is, of periodical activities in nature, human and otherwise—is the root of all significant knowledge, be it scientific or philosophical."[6]

Indeed, cyclic awareness is how we learn. With a background in nursing, I have found one nursing theorist who speaks to the pattern recognition component of cyclic awareness. Margaret Newman's nursing theory, *Health as Expanding Consciousness*[7], teaches that when a crisis arises, chaos ensues and out of this chaos comes a new organizing principle that takes our consciousness higher.

Although Newman does not identify as an astrologer, she sites Andrew M. Young's work in her book and uses a graphic of "Young's spectrum of the evolution of consciousness." This graphic reflects exactly the pattern of a lunar cycle, from "potential freedom" representing a New Moon to "binding," representative of the Second Quarter. "Centering" is represented with the Gibbous phase, "choice" with the Full Moon, "decentering" with the Disseminating phase, "unbinding" with the Fourth Quarter, and "real freedom" with the Balsamic phase.[8]

This is the pattern of cyclic awareness: we start with the New Moon, new beginning, we grow into maturity, and then we start the descent again. This ever-repeating beginning, learning, ending. Each lunar cycle, in both the Personal and Collective rhythms, has the potential of taking us to higher consciousness if we work with the rhythmic cycling in conscious awareness.

Newman also quotes Ken Wilber in her book when she writes, "Wilber saw the emergence of the human being's consciousness as separate from the world as a stage of development in which duality existed. The meaning of the development process is the transcendence of the separate self into super consciousness, a return to the wholeness of the Absolute, and with it the end of the tyranny of time."[9]

This is exactly what I propose as the benefit of consciously aligning with natural cycles, and the teaching meaning behind my business tag line, "Body as Timer." When we bear witness to these natural cycles in direct connection with our energy levels, and we, through practice, practice, practice, observe, the zero point, the infinite at the root of any duality, we do transcend separateness and fuse with wholeness, connection, or in Wilber's reference, super consciousness.

When we align High Self/Whole Self with the natural world, in this case, our Moon, we do transcend time. We open to the fluidity of cycles, to flow, the continual spiraling of increasing awareness of our circumstances and choices, free of limitation, as Young's theory implies.

These are heady words, and at heart, this paper is about feeling. Feeling the cycles as live energy flow within us and allowing this alignment to be our North Star, our Anchor, our Compass. We can get out of our heads and into our bodies with this practice of Body as Timer, in sync with Cosmic Flow.

We knew this, we did this, we used to live like this. The theosophists remind us, "Such rhythmically vibrational activity is the embodied(ed.) (imbodied) expression of the movement of cosmic intelligence...in short, cycles are the inherent rhythms of life."[10]

William Q. Judge writes in *Cyclic Impression and Return*[11] that "The esoteric doctrine, the inner doctrine, to be found in every old literature and religious book, is that cyclic law is the supreme law governing our evolution."

The direct experience of cycles, then, as felt and acknowledged through our physical bodies, is important. Our Moon is a most valuable resource for this kind of human/nature living.

Experiential Teaching

Based on my direct experience of the reliability of the Personal Lunar cycle as a predictor of energy levels, I started teaching it at places like day spas and nursing staff workshops. I teach experientially and include didactic, relaxation and guided imagery components. Over the years, I have found the relaxation component to be the most important part of this teaching process. The results suggest to me that we carry the information of our Sun/Moon birth phase within us. Going deep enough in relaxation helps access this inner knowing.

The participants at these teachings are usually women who want to know more about their connection with the Moon; they are not necessarily interested in astrology and most had not ever had their chart read and are unaware, consciously, of their lunar phase at birth.

The relaxation section involves a head to toe relaxation that takes 30-40 minutes. The guided imagery involves a journey from birth through childhood, teen years, young adult and present age that explores relationship to the Moon in the night sky. Basically, the experiential journey explores the phase of the Moon that participants see in the night sky through the guided imagery progression of these ages.

At the end of the didactic, relaxation and guided imagery sections, participants have a paper with an eight section, lunar phase wheel. They mark where they intuited their birth phase to be on this wheel.

I have taught this class approximately 25 times to groups of three to 30 people. Consistently, people intuit the phase of the Moon in which they were born. In the few cases when people did not intuit their natal lunar phase, the relaxation component of the teaching was not deep enough to open inner connection. Sometimes, if people were born at a Quarter Moon phase, they might have the wrong Quarter phase, however, they got that it is a Quarter phase.

The Lunar Cycle and Erikson's Eight Stages

As I am teaching to people who do not know astrology, I include information on the lunar cycle within the didactic portion of the workshop. A frame of reference that I use for the eight Lunar phases is Erikson's Theory of the Eight Stages of Human Growth and Development.[12]

This theory was ingrained in nursing education at the time I was training to become a nurse. Somehow, this nursing education and my astrology experience of living the lunar cycle rhythm came together.

I saw direct correlation between Erik Erikson's Eight Stages of Human Growth and Development Theory and the eight phases of the Moon, particularly in reflection of the charts of people whom I knew well. I have checked directly with the Eric H. Erikson Institute[13] inquiring into whether Erikson ever made the correlation between his theory and the lunar phases and the response I received was no.

From my perspective, there is a crossover and his theory provides a handy frame of reference for sharing with people the focus, purpose and orientation of each lunar phase from the perspective of human life. The words under the column title "Imprint" in Table 1 reflect my understanding of the functions of the phase.

Summary

It is my working hypothesis that we go through this age-related human growth and development cycle with each lunation in the Collective Lunar Cycle. It is also my working hypothesis that each native has a Sun-Moon phase angle imprint that follows them throughout the life span. This imprint is reflected in both a life focus and an energy pattern. In the Personal Lunar Cycle, the native's Sun-Moon phase angle is the New Moon starting point.

An example of the life lens imprint of lunar birth phase: Every person with a Second Quarter Moon phase whom I have read for, or gotten to know, has challenged authority—some to the extent of declining to pay taxes and others to the extent of consistently challenging status quo.

Table 1. Erikson's Psychosocial Stages Summary Chart and Aureal Williams Moon Phase Imprints

Lunar Phase	Degrees in 360 Cycle	Imprint	Erikson's Stage	Task
New Moon	0-45 degrees	Equates with infancy; formless to form, instinctual; open to all possibilities, willing, eager, curious	Psychosocial Stage 1	Trust versus Mistrust
Crescent	45-90 degrees	Equates with childhood, formation of boundaries; tension of external resistance, Self/other delineation, filtering, development of objectivity	Psychosocial Stage 2	Autonomy versus Shame and Doubt
Second Quarter	90-135 degrees	Equates with teen years; decisive action; breaking away, differentiation, instinctive, emotionally growing	Psychosocial Stage 3	Initiative versus Guilt
Gibbous	135-180 degrees	Equates with young adult age. Maturation with increasing energy of potential; inner questioning persistently refines path	Psychosocial Stage 4	Industry versus Inferiority
Full Moon	180-225 degrees	Equates with adult age. Crisis of choice, yes or no to full alignment of mind/body/spirit fusion	Psychosocial Stage 5	Identity versus Role Confusion

Disseminating	225-270 degrees	Equates with mature adult. Accepts responsibility of reciprocity, giving back or alienation, separation	Psychosocial Stage 6	Intimacy versus Isolation
Fourth Quarter	270-315 degrees	Equates with late adulthood. Tension of internal resistance: Evolutionary, transcends rejection and accepts dissolution of form back to formlessness or personalizes rejection and fears death	Psychosocial Stage 7	Generativity versus Stagnation
Balsamic	315-360 degrees	Equates with old age. Perceptive beyond the veil. Honor. Knowing without knowing, beyond mind.	Psychosocial Stage 8	Ego Integrity versus Despair

While it is helpful to know, and align with, the cyclic rhythm of both the Collective and Personal Lunar Cycles, it is also helpful to know the phase function at the point where we jump into the cycle. This overlay of lunar phase and a psychosocial organizing theory helps the native understand Self within the world. It is one other pattern identification piece to understanding life destiny and fulfillment.

Spouses, parents, employers and coworkers can benefit from an understanding of lunar phase imprints. One benefit to family life comes through a parenting perspective of the child's functional view of life according the functional role of the lunar birth phase.

The Personal Lunar Cycle rhythm reveals for parents information on the child's energy level and offers an understanding of attitude of pleasantness or grumpiness, talkativeness or sullenness and cooperation or resistance to chore completion. Parents can lower expectations during naturally occurring low energy times and offer support that enhances comfort during Dark Moon times, in both Personal and Collective Cycles.

Integrating Personal and Collective Cycles

A next step is to working with the Personal Lunar Cycle is to integrate that rhythm with the Collective Cycle. For those born within 45 degrees, before or after, a New Moon, this alignment is relatively easy, as the Dark Moon in the Personal Cycle aligns closely with the Dark Moon in the Collective Cycle. A native born near a New Moon will have a naturally occurring low energy time anywhere from three to six days corresponding to a New Moon. In these cases, there is a double strength gravitational pull to stillness with the overlay of Personal and Collective Cycles.

For those natives born in other phases, there can be a stop and start pattern to the rhythmic pattern of their energy level in relation to the Collective and Personal Dark Moon times. For instance, someone born at the Full Moon has a stop start with the Collective New Moon and another two weeks later for the Personal Cycle stop start, Dark Moon/New Moon as the natal phase angle returns each lunation.

Another example is someone born in the Second Quarter phase has the slowdown of Dark Moon in the Collective Cycle, then energy builds up again with the New Moon and then deflates again with the Dark Moon in the Personal Lunar Cycle. It is the same down, up, down, up pattern with the other Sun-Moon phases.

I have seen through my work with this natural cycle that the Personal Cycle has a more profound pull to stillness than the Collective Cycle. It seems the Personal Cycle is subtler because it is individual, however, it also seems more potent, particularly for those born in a waning Moon. The nature of the waning half of the Lunar Cycle is toward dissolution. Those natives born during a waxing Moon, in my experience, do not feel the need to come to a complete stop during a Personal Dark Moon; there is a slowdown, however, in contrast to waning Moon natives, this release and renewal phase of a Personal Dark Moon does not have the leveling effect as a native waning Moon does.

While no official, quantitative research has yet been done on the Personal Lunar Cycle, it is my working hypothesis that the application of this information can have positive impact on people dealing with chronic disease conditions. When such a person knows that she is in a naturally occurring low energy time, she can divert thoughts that the health condition is worsening; she can use this information in a predictive planning way, to keep a minimal schedule, for instance, during a Dark Moon phase in either the Personal or Collective Lunar Cycle rhythms.

Documentation

I have consistently followed this pattern in my own life since I "recovered" it in 1995. Honouring this rhythm through conscious planning and scheduling is at the core of my life. I know what happens when I do not follow it. When I do not slow down, stop, rest, retreat during the Personal Dark Moon, an irritability, a completely out of sorts, depression-like experience follows. I pay attention even though the world challenges those of us who adhere like glue to natures' rhythms. It is the Astrologer's Lament; what seems so logical, and sacred, to us, has long been forgotten.

I first wrote about The Personal Lunar Cycle under my previous name, Samten Williams, in *The Mountain Astrologer*, June/July 1999 issue. It remains available online as an Editor's Choice article.[14]

Over the years, I have taken to documenting in my blog[15] direct experiences living with the Personal Lunar Cycle. Excerpts from those articles follow. In my first blog post, titled "*Welcome*"[16] and dated June 11, 2011, I wrote:

> "The expressed intention of this blog is to share my process of living the intuitive life. The main tool that I have for this is alignment with natural cycles. My most practiced affinity is with the lunar cycles, both the collective, from New to Full Moon and the end of the lunar cycle and the Personal Lunar Cycle, which is a pattern of energy based on the phase of the Moon in which you are born.

> "In both cycles, there is a dark of the moon phase that occurs three days before the New Moon. Energy is naturally low during dark moon times and the work is on the inside. These highly receptive times are perfect for rest and reflection. . . . In my tracking, I find that alignment with the lunar cycle,

resting when it's time to be still and moving when it is time to move, lessens frustration, irritability and maybe even depression. There is a price to pay for pushing upstream in a downstream time. Every cell in our being goes through a rest phase and so do the cosmic cycles. Why not our full consciousness, the whole of our being?"

The following are excerpts from a post[17] dated May 14, 2012 when I wrote about an experience during my Dark Moon in the personal cycle:

"I can share with you that there is almost always a struggle to rest with the Dark Moon Phase. Either there is internal resistance to rest, or an external struggle to rest that comes from obstacles or judgements of others around us. In our society and culture, rest is not an authentic activity. As hard as it is to listen and acquiesce when our bodies and nature call us to rest, the consequences of not doing so affect mental, physical, emotional and spiritual health and well-being. We cannot push upstream in a downstream time and not pay for it with body, mind and soul."

From a blog post dated June 13, 2012[18]:

"In the recent dark moon phase, just preceding my Personal New Moon, I still took to the bed. I schedule the 24 hours before my Personal New Moon as a sacred time, a time for rest and relaxation and I treasure this time. Despite 17 years of faithfully following this cycle, my mind still comes in during a dark moon day shouting, "Shouldn't you . . . blah, blah, blah." I let myself rest. This recent Dark Moon phase was mostly a conscious listening time and I allowed myself the space and stillness to do that.

"Alignment with natural cycles allows us to connect consciously with the stop and start points of the cyclical nature of life. It allows us to regroup."

An excerpt about the Personal Dark Moon from my blog post dated December 7, 2012,[19] follows:

"With the dark Moon in the personal lunar cycle, there seems to be a homecoming of sorts; of information and experiences settling in as one cycle completes and the next cycle is about to begin. As the torus shape shows us, there is continual unfolding, circle upon circle. In a torus, the edges are softer, rounder, folding over into one's self for a distinct experience of completion, continued. That is what the moon's cycles do, too."

On January 11, 2016, in *The Power of a Fresh Start*[20], I referenced the integration pattern of my Personal Lunar with the Collective Lunar Cycle. Documentation excerpts from this blog post include:

"I feel the energy of the ebb and flow of natural cycles within my body as an inescapable experience. My personal dark moon phase comes about a week before the collective dark moon phase. With this pattern, there is a slowdown, then reenergizing followed soon by another downward pull and then a breakthrough new beginning.

"I love these experiences of acknowledging my body's rhythms in connection with nature's rhythms. While it is hard to resist the conditioned habit to keep going, I have learned over the years that I am better off aligning with this gravitational pull. When I don't align with it, I place undue stress on my physicality. I have learned to acquiesce to rest when the pull to rest is strong. This is how I understand self-care."

In a blog post Sacred Timing[21] dated October 27, 2016, I wrote about observing the Dark Moon phase in the Personal Cycle after that phase had ended:

> "Not everyone feels this timing. It can start with a nudge, a pull toward stillness, reflection, rest, quiet. If you sense any of this, please open the invitation. The more we align with natural, cyclic timing, the more the experience becomes familiar to us. Like all new skill sets, when we pay attention, we open receptor pathways of the original blueprints that our bodies are timers.
>
> "I anticipate the personal dark Moon phase as a sacred holiday. This is a time when I honour the whole of my life in synchronized flow with our living Universe. For us, on Earth, flow means the Moon is involved.
>
> "I have been aligning with this sacred timing since 1995. For 95% of this time, I have planned and scheduled around this pivotal timing. I have minimized commitments, laid low, and observed sensate release and regeneration typical of cyclic endings and beginnings.
>
> "Seven years ago, I took a nursing job on a per diem basis, even though I worked fulltime. I choose to forego benefits like paid time off so that I could control my schedule and not have to work on low energy Personal Dark Moon days. There is predictive value in knowing this rhythm, and I used it for self-care and well-being, and to optimize the potent receptivity (intuition, inner knowing, coming to center) inherent during Dark Moon times.
>
> "This past Personal Lunar Cycle, though, I was under deadline for a high-pressured, freelance writing assignment and I had to work through the low ener-

gy time. Eliminating distractions, cancelling social plans and staying focused on the writing task, I did muster the stamina to complete the task. It took all that I had, energetically and emotionally.

"The carrot at the end of the stick was that I knew the Moon was void of course all day on Monday, enhancing my ability to rest post project. My schedule was clear and I gave myself a do-nothing day. It was calm, sweet, comfortable, quiet, relaxing and restorative.

"On Tuesday, I was aware of still needing a little slower down time and I eased into the day with that awareness, of being kind with myself.

"I have been through enough of these Personal Lunar Cycle turnings to know that if I do not stop and be still during this precious, sacred time, a depression, an irritability, an out of sorts experience shows up. It is the beast in nature; if we do not feed the beast what it needs, in this case rest and quiet, it roars in ugliness.

"I did not get the stillness that I needed during my Personal Dark Moon, however, I knew enough to not continue forward before taking deep rest. I was a little off schedule; however, I still gave myself the self-care and stillness that I needed.

"Our bodies benefit from these rest and reset times daily, twice within the Lunar Cycle, one Personal, one Collective, and yearly, right before our birthday, with our Solar Return."

Conclusion

The phase of the Moon in which we are born carries an imprint that follows throughout life. One aspect of this imprint is a life lens that is determined by the functional aspect of the natal lunar phase. Another aspect of this life-long imprint is the rhythmic pattern of energy, based on the cyclic return of the Sun/Moon phase angle during each lunation. In the Personal Lunar Cycle, the Sun-Moon phase angle represents the New Moon. This repeating rhythm is predictable and consistent.

Using this Lunar alignment as part of one's self-care in planning and scheduling brings spiritual, creative, communal and physical benefits. Aligning with nature, feeling the Earth/Moon/Body connection as direct experience actives awareness that we belong, are part of, and are not alone.

A tiny percentage of the billions of people who live on our one Earth, embraced by the Moon, follow the Lunar Cycle as a predictable, informing energy pattern. An even smaller number of that population follows the inherent, also predictable, Personal Lunar Cycle which directs a pattern of energy based on the phase of the Moon in which one is born. Some astrologers may have resonance with this information; for those who do, this is an open call to gather; to collect more data and to help spread the word of this viscerally experienced natural cycle to others who can benefit from knowing and aligning with ourselves and Moon in this way.

From a qualitative research perspective, based on 21 years of consistently tracking this cycle in my own life and the lives of those close to me, I find the Personal Lunar Cycle has validity. I welcome community and collaborators in further research on the Personal Lunar Cycle.

Endnotes
[1] *Cycles in Nature and the Fate of the Human Soul*, no author identified, http://www.teosofia.com/Mumbai/7211cycles.html.
[2] Zebrowski , Armin, *Cycles: The Eternal Impulse of Nature*, http://www.theosophy-nw.org/theosnw/cycles/cy-azeb.htm.
[3] Ibid.

[4]Scott J. Osterhage, Scott J. *Inherent Rhythms of Life*, http://www.theosophy-nw.org/theosnw/cycles/cy-oste.htm.
[5]Pessin, Dietrech Lunar Shadows http://www.lunar-shadows.com/my-book.
[6]Rudyhar, Dane http://beyondsunsigns.com/rudhyarcycles.html
[7]Newman, Margaret, 1999, Health as Expanding Consciousness, New York, National League of Nursing Press.
[8]Ibid, p. 44.
[9]Ibid, p. 43.
[10]de Purucke, G, Causative Nature of Cycles http://theosophy-nw.org/theosnw/cycles/cy-gdp2.htm.
[11]de Purucke, G, Causative Nature of Cycles http://theosophy-nw.org/theosnw/cycles/cy-gdp2.htm.
[12]Erikson's Psychosocial Stages http://www.simplypsychology.org/Erik-Erikson.html.
[13]Erik H. Erikson Institute http://www.erikson.edu/about/history/erik-erikson/ private email correspondence.
[14]Williams, Samten, June/July 1999, *The Mountain Astrologer* http://www.mountainastrologer.com/standards/editor's%20choice/articles/lunar_cycles/lunar_cycles.html.
[15]Williams, Aureal, Living the Intuitive Life, www.aurealwilliams.com/blog.
[16]Williams, Aureal, Welcome" June 11, 2011, http://aurealwilliams.com/blog/welcome/.
[17]Williams, Aureal, Personal Dark Moon, May, 14 2012. http://aurealwilliams.com/blog/personal-dark-moon-may-2012-experience/.
[18]Williams, Aureal, Personal Lunar Cycle, June 13, 2012, http://aurealwilliams.com/blog/personal-dark-moon-june-2012-experience/.
[19]Williams, Aureal, Personal Dark Moon, December 7, 2012, http://aurealwilliams.com/blog/personal-dark-moon-december-8-2012/
[20]Williams, Aureal, January 11, 2016, The Power of a Fresh Start, http://aurealwilliams.com/blog/the-power-of-a-fresh-start/
[21]Williams, Aureal Sacred Timing October 27, 2016, http://aurealwilliams.com/blog/sacred-timing/.

Bibliography

Newman, Margaret, Newman, Margaret, 1999, *Health as Expanding Consciousness*, New York, National League of Nursing Press.

Domestic Terrorism: 2016 Was a Difficult Year

By Marilyn J. Muir, LPMAFA

ABSTRACT: Our world has been experiencing multiple and major acts of international terrorism for many years. More recently, high numbers of domestic terrorism are on the rise, wherein citizens of a country identify or train with international terrorist groups to attack within their own country. In September 2016, the U.S. was subjected to three such attacks within one day, with another attack six days later. Research into the four-event grouping identified common degrees that had joined major long-range stress aspects such as Uranus square Pluto in cardinal signs and Saturn square Neptune in mutable signs. Further research for those degree areas identified the attack in Orlando, Florida. Even further research included several other much older acts of domestic terrorism involving those same common degrees: the World Trade Center 9/11 attack, the Oklahoma City bombing, and the Boston Marathon bombing. Commonality of degree areas were verified in all those events. Additionally, solar and lunar eclipses just prior to each event were investigated as potential triggers to those degree areas and included in the findings of this research project.

On September 17, 2016 three acts of domestic terrorism erupted . . . in Seaside Park, New Jersey, Chelsea district in Manhattan, New York, and St. Cloud, Minnesota. Six days later, in Burlington, Washington, another attack. Why? Since they were close together in time, there will be some commonality in degree positions and aspects. What can we learn by studying that commonality? Starting with an overview. . . .

Our world daily turns (rotates and orbits) within a solar system orbital energy pattern that affects all parts of the world, all cultures, all clusters of population, all religions, all politics, all life. If we look around our world at countries, cultures, and populations we can see similar energy patterns activating all over the globe. Such cosmic patterns are not local or personal; they are worldwide. As humans, we tend to take our local viewpoint and make it personal. We are affected and infected when it becomes personal.

The Uranus in Aries square Pluto in Capricorn pattern that has held the world hostage for the last few years continues by separating orb. The fact that the pattern is no longer applying does not seem to explain why the affiliated nonsense is continuing. Why? The activating principle of the applying aspect did its job. It initiated or developed the dynamics of the acute, crisis-oriented, cardinal square between the planet of disruption, attention-getting headlines, breaking through existing barriers Uranian energy and the underground, psychological, collective unconscious Plutonian energy. Our human collective psychological underbelly was exposed into full worldview. Does that sound anything like what has been going on recently?

How big an orb should be allowed for this world-changing aspect? Closer to perfect is stronger; anything wider and applying represents the process leading up to the critical phase of the aspect or its developmental cycle. Once perfected, the initiatory phase is complete and the cycle swings into application of what has been initiated, the separating phase. We are no longer in the formation process; we are then in the implementation process. The energy of the square still exists but now it is expressing what has already been initiated. The aspect did not just go away because it completed itself; it is now wearing a different face . . . that of ongoing worldwide events, some of which have become personal because they are local.

As difficult as this seems, this one energy pattern is not alone; world-shaping aspects do not necessarily occur one at a time. We have also been experiencing Saturn in Sagittarius square Neptune in Pisces, a difficult, hard aspect within a personal chart that is described as the "dark night of the soul." As hard as that may seem when active in one's individual life, how much more difficult is it when experienced by us all as the world rotates and orbits through that difficult energy dynamic? These patterns exist for all of us collectively and it turns personal when it affects our individual charts. It also turns personal when it affects our country's chart, our city's chart, and all individually cast charts that happen to get activated by such a worldwide aspect.

Look around at what is happening in this world. It is difficult to believe what is happening to us. We are horrified by the examples we are presented with across the world. Our faith in ourselves and in humanity is being tested. What is real in an unreal world? What is real in our country, our political structures, our towns and cities, in our homes and our lives? The Saturn-Neptune square is difficult on any level, and at times it gets personal. The degree-to-degree activation of Saturn on Neptune is nine months, but that does not take into account applying orb and separating orb. As I write this we are now in separating aspect but still within orb. We have moved from initiation to application, and this aspect continues until the energy peters out. Just do not become complacent at that point, because the energy did come into being and now exists as a part of our lives.

Those are the two major patterns our world is experiencing, but astrologically there is always more to see. . . .

We are about to examine four events as acts of domestic terrorism. I looked up the subject, and found that Wikipedia has a U.S. terrorism list going back into the 1800s. We do know it goes back further than that. When Europeans first discovered the Caribbean Islands and America there were indigenous people who would have looked at the explorers as invaders, and those same explorers proved the natives were right. Their lands, cultures, and societies were taken from them, first by sword and gun, but also by infectious disease. It was as invasive, as devastating, and as horrific as what we call terrorism today, very similar in application and effect to the people of that day and age. Once the settling was underway, European nations fought each other and their settlers for ownership of the new territory. The native occupants either participated with one country or another or became further victims. The succeeding generations of explorers/settlers were continually defending/expanding. Whether you were a good guy or a bad guy depended on your personal perspective. Whether or not you were born on this soil is irrelevant to the victims.

Suffice it to say there has been other domestic terrorism; it is not new to our shores. The latest perceived obscenity has been Americans attacking Americans on American soil. Just know this is not new or a sign of our times; it is age old. The form or name has changed, but human destruction continues. Our original Revolutionary War was fought within families and friends as well as with and within the existing British political structure. Our Civil War was fought not only between North and South, but between families and friends. Each side would operate from a personal perspective as to who were the heroes and who were adversaries.

Three of the four events selected occurred September 17, 2016, accurately timed for our purposes.

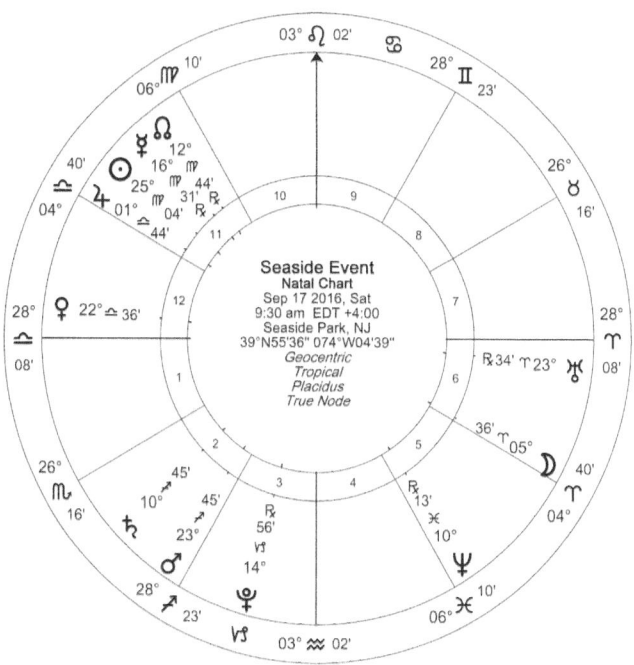

Seaside Park, New Jersey

The Seaside Semper Five Marathon at Seaside Park, New Jersey bomb explosion occurred at 9:30 a.m. (9:35 first police report). Using the 9:30 a.m. chart we will focus on the two major patterns described above. We will use hard aspects only to illustrate such a horrific possibility. It is my experience that soft aspects illustrate the relative ease of the perpetrators for hiding in plain sight. This conclusion was gleaned from many years studying the charts of serial killers.

- Chart ruler Venus at 22 Libra 37 occupies the twelfth house of sabotage or hidden enemies opposition retrograde Uranus at 23 Aries 35 in the sixth house. In my experience, sixth-twelfth house activations show frequently in psychologically driven acts. Venus also *rules* the twelfth house of sabotage or hidden enemies *plus* the eighth house of catastrophe. Uranus rules the fourth house of end of the matter and the grave. Venus and Uranus are in very wide separating square to retrograde Pluto at 14 Capricorn 57 in the third house of local travel and communication. Again, the Uranus-Pluto square is in the separating or implementation stage of seeds planted during its initiating phase.

- Retrograde Mercury of communication at 16 Virgo 31 conjunction the retrograde North Node at 12 Virgo 45 in the eleventh house of groups and associations is opposition retrograde Neptune at 10 Pisces 13 conjunction the South Node in the fifth house of pleasure and personal competition, all square Saturn at 10 Sagittarius 46 in the second house of personal values, ruling both the third and fourth houses as previously given. In my experience the lunar nodes are frequently found in charts with a fated or destiny connotation.

- The Midheaven (mission) is 3 Leo 02, ruled by the Sun at 25 Virgo 05 in the eleventh of groups and associations, square Mars at 23 Sagittarius 45 occupying the second of house personal values with Mars ruling the seventh house of other people or open enemies. The good news is that the race had a late start so no one was hurt. Two other bombs were placed at nearby locations but did not detonate. Although this is considered an event, no casualties were reported. This explosion did initiate the day's events.

Manhattan, New York

The Manhattan explosion took place eleven hours later at 8:31 p.m. in the very popular dinner/entertainment Chelsea district, with hundreds of people enjoying an autumn evening. Other explosive devices were also found in the general area but had not exploded. From both New Jersey and New York there were several other events, but we will stay with the two deliberate explosions. It was later found that one person or-

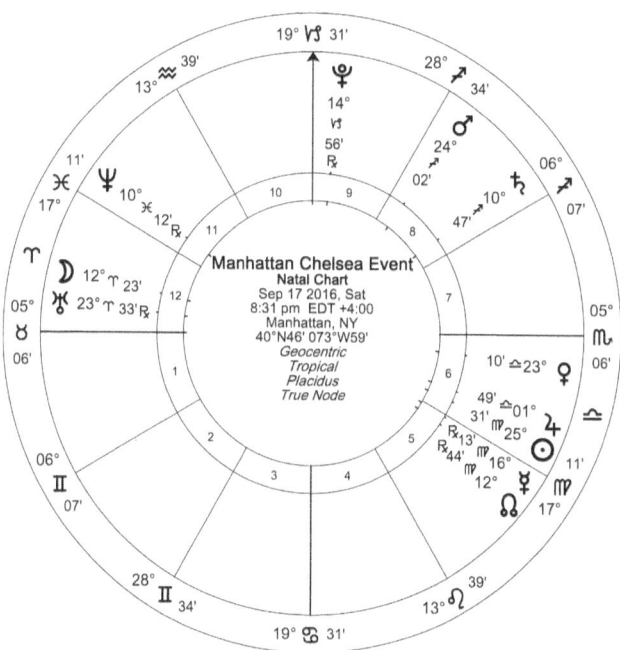

ganized and committed all the events in both states; however this investigation is ongoing.

- This time 5 Taurus 06 was rising, again Venus-ruled. However the chart had nearly reversed. The Venus-Uranus opposition was still in charge but Venus was intercepted in the sixth and Uranus was intercepted in the twelfth. Both were in wide separating square to Pluto which now was on the ninth-house side of the Midheaven. The Midheaven at 19 Capricorn 32 was in applying square to that opposition. This chart was controlled by the motion of the angle (more active) and did physical damage as injuries to people and property. The Moon had now moved to 12 Aries 24, closely square Pluto, technically a very potent aspect, intensifying and expanding the existing T-square.

- The Neptune-South Node conjunction opposition the Mercury-North Node conjunction was still square Saturn, degrees largely unchanged; but the house positions were vastly different. The sixth-twelfth house activations continued but with the planets and rulerships relocated. This time Neptune occupied the eleventh house of groups and associations and ruled the twelfth house of sabotage and ambush. Mercury and the South Node were in the fifth of pleasure and entertainment. The T-square established by Saturn had moved into the eighth house of catastrophe.

- The Sun-Mars square had moved to the sixth-eighth houses, joining illness-disease to catastrophe. For this explosion many were injured but with no fatalities. This strengthening T-square involved the Saturn-ruled Midheaven, a critical difference.

St. Cloud, Minnesota

The third event that occurred September 17 was a St. Cloud, Minnesota shopping mall stabbing attack with 10 victims and, fortunately, no fatalities. Wounds were to the upper part of the body and head. The assailant, Dahir Adan, was confronted and killed by an off-duty police officer. During the attack Adan shouted the name Allah and asked if some of his intended victims were Muslim. The time was 8:15 p.m. This chart becomes a good example of the purpose and value of longitude and time standards as this Midheaven falls between the two charts already examined: the Seaside Park and Manhattan explosions. Take the opportunity to look at the three charts to see the differences.

Remember the Venus-Uranus opposition that ruled the two prior charts? In this chart, that opposition lies directly on the Ascendant-Descendant axis and the square to Pluto lies on the tenth house, or applying, side of the Midheaven. Aspects directly on the angles tend to be more crisis-oriented, direct or visible. Additionally, the Moon is at 12 Aries 51 (critical degree) in this chart closely square the Midheaven and Pluto

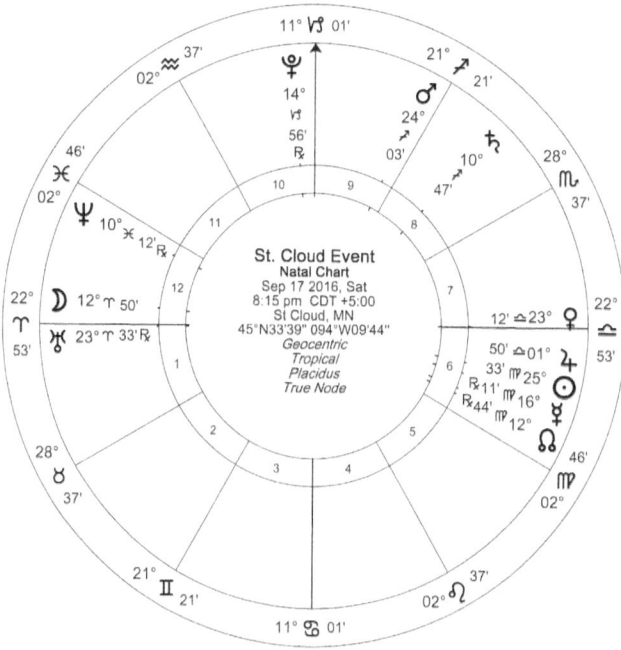

(midpoints work). The Moon rules the fourth house of homeland, foundation, and home (territory).

Uranus would qualify as a co-ruler because this chart has 22 Aries 53 rising with actual Mars at 24 Sagittarius 04 square the Sun 25 Virgo 33 in the sixth. I mentioned that the terrorist called out the name of Allah and he asked if his targets were Islamic. Mars as chart ruler is in the ninth house of religion and foreign cultural belief systems. Mars generally rules knives and in this case steak knives were the weapons of choice. Rulership counts.

Our third speculative degree area is the existing Neptune-South Node conjunction in the twelfth house opposition Mercury conjunction North Node square Saturn in the eighth house. This aspect involved the psychological sixth-twelfth house axis and the eighth house of catastrophe.

Have you noticed that only Jupiter seems to be exempt from these aspects? Go back to the first chart. The Moon was just past the opposition to Jupiter, which was at that point void of specific participation, unable to actively affect the outcome of all three charts. *Do make note that the transiting Sun moves one degree per day and it will take six days for the Sun to reach Jupiter.*

Burlington, Washington

Our fourth chart is for the Burlington, Washington, shopping mall shooting on September 23, 2016, *six days* after the three attacks already defined. The Uranus-Pluto and Saturn-Neptune aspects were still in place, but the faster-moving planets had made some changes.

- A lone man entered the shopping mall about 6:48 p.m., seemingly unarmed. The shooting itself began at 6:58 p.m. Both charts are of value because the angles changed. Mars, which figured so prominently in the previous charts, changed from angular to behind the angle. (6:46 p.m. was the last minute that Mars remained in the tenth house so I am referencing that speculative chart.) Aries is intercepted in the first so Mars is a co-ruler of the chart (interceptions delay but do not necessarily deny) and it co-rules the eighth of catastrophe and death. Mars rules guns, and the weapon of choice was a rifle. Step by step. . . .

- The Uranus-Venus opposition was widely separating and out of sign as Venus had passed into Scorpio. Uranus and Pluto were still widely square with Pluto, retrograding toward the applying opposition of the Moon at 9 Cancer 52. Is this or is this not a cardinal grand square? By degree, very wide, too wide; by application, still possible? Uranus is in the first house, Venus in the seventh, Moon in the fourth, and Pluto in the tenth, all angular, which is critical to active or visible power.

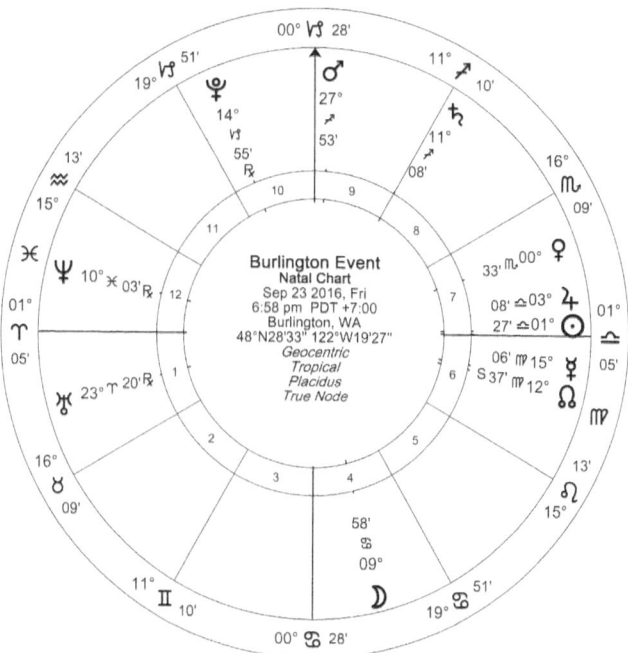

- The Neptune-South Node conjunction opposition the Mercury-North Node conjunction, all square Saturn, still exists, with Neptune now as the chart ruler in the twelfth house of ambush and sabotage. We have picked up the Sun-Jupiter conjunction in early degrees of cardinal on an out-of-sign square to Mars-Midheaven.

- At 6:58 p.m., the time the shooting started, everything changed as the Ascendant moved to 1 Aries 07 opposing the Sun at 1 Libra 27 conjunction Jupiter at 3 Libra 08, all square the Midheaven at 00 Capricorn 29 and the out-of-sign and separating chart ruler Mars at 27 Sagittarius 53. We have definitely moved from the setting of the stage to the application for that event.

Commonality of degrees and aspects holds between these charts, and the derived house descriptions match the action.

Know that each chart has other patterns as well, unique to that event. This research specifically focuses on specific degree area activation.

I also applied the September 2016 eclipses to the four events as eclipses commonly provide a trigger for major events: the solar eclipse at 9 Virgo 21 on September 1 and the lunar eclipse at 24 Pisces 19 on September 16, the day prior to the three attacks.

- 9 Virgo triggered the Saturn-Neptune-Node-Mercury T-square in all four charts.
- 24 Virgo triggered the Sun-Mars square in the three charts on September 17, and the Midheaven-Mars conjunction square Sun-Jupiter on September 23.

What about the spring eclipses? We had a horrendous example of domestic terrorism in June with the Pulse nightclub attack in Orlando, Florida, now referred to as the Orlando massacre. A lone gunman shot and killed 49 innocents at a Latino music show in a LGBT nightclub. While it might have been an LGBT attack, there were also non-LGBT music fans and venue staff in that audience; the victims were diverse. The gunman was the 50th victim. Or you might add in the senseless killing of singer Christina Grimmie the night before the Pulse nightclub attack, again at a music venue in Orlando . . . senseless, senseless, senseless.

Just how long do eclipses spread their influence? The two eclipses we first examined were immediately prior to the events. Was there a long-term effect from the spring 2016 eclipses to the four autumn events examined; such influence would represent about six months of effect.

- March 8, 2016 solar eclipse: 18 Pisces 55, between existing degree areas
- March 23, 2016 lunar eclipse: 3 Libra 17, a new degree area

The degrees we have been examining are approximately 10 and 25 degrees mutable. Now we will additionally look at 19 mutable and 3 cardinal but will keep tight orbs.

- New Jersey explosion: Moon, 5 Aries 36; Jupiter 1 Libra 44 (there it is!)
- Mercury, 16 Virgo 31 retrograde
- Manhattan explosion and Minnesota mall stabbing: again Jupiter and Mercury
- Washington mall shooting: Midheaven, 0 Capricorn 29; Ascendant, 1 Aries 07; Sun and Jupiter; Mercury, 15 Virgo 06

I had previously researched the Pulse nightclub attack, the Orlando Massacre. It is thought the initiating event was at 1:58 a.m. The spring solar eclipse definitely activated the nightclub charts:

- Sun 21 Gemini 42, Venus 23 Virgo 09, Moon 20 Virgo 41, North Node 16 Virgo 49

The lunar eclipse degree kicked in about four minutes (2:02 a.m.) after the entry, when shots were reported to the police.

- 1:58 a.m. Midheaven, 29 Sagittarius 11; Ascendant, 29 Pisces 44 (out of sign but within orb). *Note*: The horrific Orlando massacre did not occur in a moment; it occurred over a four-hour period.
- 2:02 a.m. Midheaven, 0 Capricorn 06; Ascendant, 0 Aries 10 (rulerships changed)

Looking at the two charts four minutes apart . . .

During the description of the Washington Mall shooting it was mentioned that a discrepancy existed between the time the shooter entered the mall without a weapon and the actual time the shooting started, about 10 minutes or so according to the news reports. Somewhere in those few minutes the shooter accessed a weapon, currently unanswered. Astrologically the two charts were quite different and the activities of each moment were quite different. That same thing is true of the Pulse nightclub attack, but with a much shorter time frame, about four minutes. What might have happened that would explain the discrepancy?

I reasoned that the Pulse nightclub would have closed at 2:00 a.m. per Florida law. Last service would have been called and delivered and patrons would be exiting the nightclub. Reportedly the club did check for weapons for all incoming patrons. If the patrons were leaving, it is possible that anyone *entering* would not have been checked. It would not be unusual for someone to have forgotten their cell phone, perhaps thought to have lost their keys, etc. An incoming patron would not have been suspect. In the four minutes between 1:58 and 2:02 a.m. (first call to police), the rulership of the chart changed dramatically.

At 1:58 a.m., with 28 Pisces 44 rising, ruler Neptune was in the twelfth house of subterfuge, ambush, and hidden enemies. Co-ruler Jupiter-North Node in the sixth house psychological axis opposed Neptune-South Node, complex square Saturn (sound familiar?) in the ninth house of foreign cultures or belief systems. The Moon had just crossed over the Jupiter-North Node conjunction and was square the Sun-Venus conjunction. The four angles in this chart are square each other. The Midheaven represents the pinnacle of achievement for that moment in time: 29 Sagittarius 11, also ruled by the Jupiter complex.

At 2:02 a.m., four minutes later, the Ascendant was at 0 Aries 10, with ruler retrograde Mars in the eighth house of catastrophe at 25 Scorpio 12 opposition Mercury at 29 Taurus 02 in the second house of personal values. Mars is opposite fixed star Caput Algol, the most malefic fixed star in the zodiac, read modernly as "losing one's head." Mercury is conjunct the Pleiades, the seven weeping sisters, read modernly as "something to weep about." We have gone from subterfuge to aggression, from hidden enemy to perpetrator, from intent to action . . . in four minutes.

Amazing that two supposedly unconnected events can show similar patterns and tight timing.

What about the people involved in these attacks? Do we have charts on them and what can we learn from these charts? Are the degrees represented in this article valid with the charts of the suspected assailants? Remember in the U.S. a person is considered a suspect until proven guilty by our judicial system. Trial by media or gossip is not valid and should not be tolerated in a free society. This, therefore, is speculative on my part.

The New Jersey and Manhattan attacks were thought to have been committed by one person, Ahmad Rahimi. Date and place of birth is available for Rahimi. Noonmark is used.

The Minnesota attack was carried out by Dahir A. Adan, who was killed at the scene during the event. He was born in Kenya circa 1994; date, time, or place are unavailable.

Arcan Cetin is the *suspect* for the Washington mall shooting. Date and place is available for Cetin: born August 20, 1996 in Adana, Turkey; noonmark is used.

Omar Mateen was accused in the Orlando massacre and his birth certificate with time was published by news sources. Mateen was born November 16, 1986, 7:00 p.m., Queens, New York.

Only the previously determined degree sensitivities were examined.

The New Jersey and Manhattan attacks suspect:
- Rahimi noonmark natal: Venus, 9 Pisces 18; Mars, 9 Sagittarius 47; Neptune, 8 Capricorn 37; North Node, 24 Pisces

22; Saturn, 27 Sagittarius 56; Uranus 28 Sagittarius 56
- Rahimi chart progressed: noonmark, Ascendant 19 Gemini 43; Uranus, 00 Capricorn 14; Saturn, 00 Capricorn 34
- Rahmini diurnal chart: noonmark, Ascendant 13 Sagittarius 19

The Washington attack suspect:
- Certin, noonmark natal: Mercury, 24 Virgo 55; retrograde Jupiter, 8 Capricorn 08; retrograde Saturn, 6 Aries 32; South Node, 8 Aries 39 (wide)
- Cetin chart noonmark progressed: Midheaven, 7 Virgo 23; Sun, 17 Virgo 03; retrograde Mercury, 2 Libra 03; retrograde North Node, 8 Libra 08 (axis); retrograde Saturn, 5 Aries 17; Jupiter 7 Capricorn 52 (some wide); *note:* noonmark Ascendant, 26 Scorpio 06, opposition fixed star Caput Algol
- Cetin noonmark diurnal chart: Midheaven, 22 Virgo 19; Ascendant, 7 Sagittarius 25, Saturn 11 Sagittarius 06; Moon 0 Cancer 16

Orlando Massacre suspect (timed charts):
- Mateen natal: Midheaven, 10 Pisces 23; Jupiter, 13 Pisces 06; Saturn, 10 Sagittarius 08; Uranus 20 Sagittarius 55; Ascendant, 3 Cancer 27; Neptune, 4 Capricorn 05; *note*: Moon, 29 Taurus 47 (fixed star Caput Algol)
- Mateen progressed chart: Mercury, 9 Sagittarius 33; Saturn, 13 Sagittarius 37; Mars, 14 Pisces 01; Jupiter, 15 Pisces 21; Uranus, 22 Sagittarius 40; Sun, 24 Sagittarius 18; Moon, 27 Gemini 19 (wide, out of sign); Neptune, 5 Capricorn 06
- Mateen diurnal chart: Midheaven, 7 Libra 30 (wide); Moon, 17 Virgo 40; Ascendant, 16 Sagittarius 50

There are many contacts within reasonable orb between the

assailant and associated events.

Please note noonmark Ascendant, Midheaven, and Moon are always speculative positions. Please also note there will be other pertinent aspects between these associated events and perpetrators that are outside the scope of this study.

In each of these attacks, not only the event and the perpetrator were involved. The attacks also had a direct effect on their locations. Any community whose sense of safety and well-being is threatened is terrorized and in shock, especially when there is a direct loss of residents. How does the chart of a community reflect such an event by natal, progressed, or diurnal (personal transits) charts? Such information is available should you want to dig a little deeper. Remember there is more to see in each chart pairing but we are staying focused on specific degree areas. Only the significant degree positions of Midheaven, Ascendant, and Moon are considered for diurnals (personal transits) as the balance of the planetary positions remain as previously given in the event charts. Starting with the three events of September 17, 2016:

- Seaside Park, New Jersey was incorporated May 3, 1898; noonmark is used. Natal Venus at 2 Gemini 30 is opposition retrograde Uranus at 2 Sagittarius 19 retrograde, wide, but remember the transiting Venus-Uranus opposition for the event itself; this is *aspect resonance* between the charts. Pluto at 13 Gemini 29 is opposition retrograde Saturn at 10 Sagittarius 51. Pluto is also widely conjunct Neptune at 20 Gemini 49.

- Seaside Park progressed chart: Sun, 6 Virgo 42 conjunction noonmark Midheaven, 7 Virgo 30, square Saturn, 5 Sagittarius 59; wide conjunction (stellium) contains Pluto at 15 Gemini 40, Neptune at 24 Gemini 34, Mars at 27 Gemini 39 (bridges and potentially connects two separate degree areas)

- Seaside Park diurnal chart: noonmark Midheaven, 27 Virgo 47; noonmark Ascendant, 9 Sagittarius 55; Saturn, 10 Sagittarius 46; noonmark Moon, 7 Aries 45

Can the chart of the larger community, such as the state in which the event took place, also reflect the event?

- New Jersey was granted statehood on December 18, 1787, in Trenton; noonmark is used. Natal Mercury, 7 Sagittarius 50; Sun, 26 Sagittarius 48; North Node, 26 Sagittarius 08; noonmark Midheaven, 27 Sagittarius 26; noonmark Ascendant, 25 Pisces 12; retrograde Jupiter, 20 Gemini 46 widely conjunction South Node; noonmark Moon, 7 Aries 18

- New Jersey chart progressed: Mars, 24 Virgo 51; retrograde North Node, 15 Sagittarius 24; retrograde Saturn, 9 Pisces 24

- New Jersey diurnal chart, similar to Seaside diurnal: New Jersey diurnal noonmark Ascendant, 9 Sagittarius 00.

Further, can the chart of a country reflect an event? Using the Virgo rising chart for the U.S. Declaration of Independence, July 4, 1776, 9:36 a.m., Philadelphia, Pennsylvania.

- U.S. Ascendant, 11 Virgo 46; Midheaven, 8 Gemini 52; Uranus, 8 Gemini 54; Mars, 21 Gemini 10

- U.S. progressed Sun, 11 Pisces 37; Uranus, 7 Gemini 04. *Note*: These U.S. figures apply to all the state charts for September 17, 2016 events. For other dates during 2016, only the progressing Moon changed rapidly, approximately one degree per month.

- U.S. diurnal Moon, 21 Pisces 37

These U.S. figures also apply to the following state and city charts for September 17, 2016 events.

- Manhattan, New York was incorporated February 2, 1653; noonmark is traditional; Ascendant, 4 Gemini 39; retrograde Pluto, 12 Gemini 09; North Node, 23 Pisces 04 (axis); Neptune, 23 Sagittarius 00; Uranus wide at 29 Sagittarius 17 and out of sign to 0 cardinal; Venus, 6 Capricorn 14

- Manhattan progressed chart: Ascendant, 2 Gemini 44 (360° return); retrograde North Node, 4 Pisces 09; retrograde Pluto, 13 Gemini 10; Venus, 28 Pisces 54; Uranus, 3 Capricorn 16
- Manhattan diurnal chart, similar to the Seaside Park, New Jersey figures: Midheaven, 26 Virgo 47; Ascendant, 8 Gemini 49; Moon, 7 Aries 43
- New York was granted statehood July 26, 1788 (seven months after New Jersey), noonmark traditional. Mars, 20 Virgo 02; North Node, 15 Sagittarius 47; retrograde Saturn, 9 Pisces 54
- New York progressed chart is full of mutable: Venus, 00 Pisces 58; Mars, 04 Pisces 44, wide to retrograde North Node at 01 Sagittarius 04 retrograde (axis); Saturn, 14 Pisces 32; retrograde Mercury, 16 Pisces 00; noonmark Midheaven, 19 Pisces 00; Sun, 21 Pisces 44; Moon, 25 Virgo 31
- New York diurnal similar to Seaside Park diurnal: Midheaven, 26 Virgo 47; Ascendant, 8 Gemini 40; Moon, 7 Aries 43

Apply the US. natal, progressed, and diurnal figures to these New Jersey and New York figures.

- St. Cloud, Minnesota was incorporated April 2, 1856, noonmark traditional: Moon, 8 Pisces 08; Venus, 14 Pisces 43; Neptune, 18 Pisces 49; Mercury, 21 Pisces 34; Jupiter, 22 Pisces 07; Saturn, 24 Gemini 29
- St. Cloud progressed chart: Sun, 18 Virgo 37; noonmark Midheaven, 19 Virgo 33; retrograde Neptune, 19 Pisces 02; Ascendant, 00 Sagittarius 27 (wide)

- St. Cloud diurnal chart: Midheaven, 26 Virgo 51; Ascendant, 5 Sagittarius 39; Moon, 8 Aries 33 (wide)
- Minnesota was granted statehood May 11, 1858; St. Paul was the capital: Venus, 9 Gemini '03; retrograde North Node, 15 Pisces 40
- Minnesota progressed chart: Venus, 9 Sagittarius 23; North Node, 7 Pisces 43; retrograde Neptune, 22 Pisces 43; retrograde Jupiter, 21 Gemini 32; retrograde Uranus, 2 Gemini 52 retrograde (wide)
- Minnesota diurnal similar to St. Cloud diurnal: Midheaven, 26 Virgo 51; Ascendant, 6 Sagittarius 04; Moon, 8 Aries 30

Apply the U.S. natal, progressed and diurnal figures to these state figures.

This completes the comparison of the September 17, 2016 events to their city, state, and country charts. Particularly, the sensitive mutable degrees are all activated. Always read a more current chart *to* an earlier dated chart for activations. Next, this same comparison will be done for the September 23 event in Washington state.

- Burlington, Washington incorporation June 18, 1902, noonmark traditional: Mars, 8 Gemini 02; Pluto, 18 Gemini 22; Midheaven, 14 Gemini 19; retrograde Uranus, 18 Sagittarius; Sun, 26 Gemini 37; Ascendant, 25 Virgo 28; Neptune, 1 Cancer 00; retrograde Mercury, 4 Cancer 09
- Burlington progressed charts: Ascendant, 18 Sagittarius 47; Uranus, 18 Sagittarius 06; retrograde Pluto, 19 Gemini 37; Venus, 4 Libra 29; retrograde Neptune, 3 Cancer 43

Burlington diurnal chart: Ascendant, 6 Sagittarius 24; Midheaven, 0 Libra 51; Moon, 6 Cancer 35

- Washington was granted statehood November 11, 1889, capital Olympia, noonmark traditional. Saturn, 2 Virgo 57; retrograde Neptune, 3 Gemini 32; retrograde Pluto,

6 Gemini 14; Mars, 0 Libra 32; Jupiter, 6 Capricorn 56; Moon, 5 Cancer 57; North Node, 3 Cancer 42 (axis) (some wide)

- Washington progressed chart: Midheaven, 22 Pisces 41; Sun, 28 Pisces 04; retrograde North Node, 28 Gemini 37 (axis); Mercury, 9 Pisces 15; Neptune, 2 Gemini 07; Pluto, 5 Gemini 06; Mars, 6 Sagittarius 38; Venus, 5 Aries 02
- Washington diurnal similar to Burlington diurnal.

Apply the previously given U.S. natal, progressed, and diurnal figures to these state figures. Six days of yearly progression do not significantly move the positions.

The same technique applies to the Orlando massacre.

- Pulse Nightclub incorporation May 19, 2003, 8:00 a.m. (time stamp), Tallahassee, Florida; Midheaven, 0 Pisces 23 conjunction Uranus 2 Pisces 41 (within orb); Ascendant, 17 Sagittarius 53; retrograde Pluto, 19 Sagittarius 00; Saturn, 28 Gemini 05 (out of sign square to cardinal)
- Pulse chart progressed: Midheaven, 14 Pisces 05; Sun, 10 Gemini 40; Uranus, 2 Pisces 48 (wide), Ascendant, 00 Cancer 05; Moon, 26 Gemini 02; Saturn, 29 Gemini 41; retrograde Pluto, 18 Sagittarius 49
- Pulse diurnal chart: Midheaven, 26 Pisces 41; repeating planets for event: Sun at 21 Gemini 57, Venus at 23 Gemini 28, Moon at 23 Virgo 43, Jupiter at 14 Virgo 56, retrograde North Node at 16 Virgo 49 (axis), Neptune at 12 Pisces 02; Saturn 12 Sagittarius 26 retrograde
- Orlando, Florida incorporation, July 31, 1875, Orlando, noonmark traditional. Mars 21 Sagittarius 37.
- Orlando progressed chart: Mercury, 23 Sagittarius 30; Sun, 27 Sagittarius 20; Midheaven, 27 Sagittarius 57; Ascendant, 26 Pisces 48; Moon, 27 Virgo 00; retrograde North Node, 4 Aries 31 (axis)

- Orlando diurnal chart: Midheaven, 22 Gemini 10; Ascendant, 22 Virgo 29; Moon, 26 Virgo 26
- Florida statehood occurred March 3, 1845, Tallahassee, noonmark traditional. Midheaven, 9 Pisces 48; Sun, 13 Pisces 03; Ascendant, 26 Gemini 25; Mars, 26 Sagittarius 50; Uranus, 4 Aries 54
- Florida progressed chart: Venus, 25 Virgo 01; Mercury, 25 Virgo 03
- Florida diurnal chart for massacre: similar to Orlando diurnal.
- U. S. chart progressed comparison, see September 17 listing above for most positions: Moon, three degrees earlier than mid-September at 29 Scorpio 46 opposition fixed star Pleiades, "something to weep about."
- U. S. diurnal comparison: Moon at 25 Virgo 02, other planets listed see Orlando diurnal positions.

Please know that other domestic terrorism events and perpetrators do reflect the degree areas presented here: the Boston Marathon bombing, the 9/11 World Trade Center attacks, and the Oklahoma City bombing. I invite more research showing the commonality. Perhaps hindsight can lead us to foresight in this dangerous age.

Conclusion

Our world has been subjected to major difficult energy patterns for many years. In 2008-9 our current worldwide political pattern was subjected to the Saturn/Uranus opposition and our world reeled under the impact of conservative versus progressive energy on all levels of the world stage. We are still living under the effects of that pattern. More recently Uranus has been in square to Pluto for many years, and the bizarre extremes of action are self-evident. More recently we experienced Saturn square Neptune with truth and lies permeating our experience worldwide. As the faster moving planets and the eclipses moved in and out of those existing major patterns, brutal events occurred and world political structures and economies suffered. For most of 2016 the inner planets transiting mutable and cardinal signs triggered those major stress patterns, with only occasional relief from the stability implied by fixed signs. The world has been in chaos as cardinal energies initiate and mutable energies flex and adapt, with little to no stability from fixed.

The Saturn-Uranus opposition centered on the 20th degree of mutable (Virgo-Pisces), setting the stage for the 2008 U.S. election and the 2009 inauguration. In 2010 the world experienced Saturn square Pluto, Libra in Capricorn, and the drive for power and control centered in the early degrees. Right behind that was Uranus moving into Libra for its confrontation also with Pluto as Saturn completed its passage. Saturn opposed Uranus both squared Pluto was the world stage. All countries experienced this as the governing energy for that time, in very early cardinal. Then Neptune moved into early mutable (Pisces) and waited for Saturn to wend its way to Sagittarius which it did at the very end of 2014. Saturn and Neptune danced their square until late in 2016, early to mid-mutable, and the world did a terrible dance on so many levels. Early mutable, early cardinal and 20 degrees of mutable show up in every chart from the 1995 Oklahoma City bombing, 2001 World Trade Center bombing, 2013 Boston Marathon and the 2016 grouping of five U.S. events researched. That does not take into consideration all the worldwide events such as France, the Middle East, Belgium, too many to enumerate. Those events occurred under the same pattern, localized but not less devastating. It became a hope that identifying such degree areas from our past might be useful to note upcoming potential violence. Prevention may not be possible; but identification might help.

Chart Data

Event sources: Multiple current and continuing news reports and articles were used as the events unfolded, constantly changing, Wikipedia articles are an updated synopsis and timeline combined, with major individual citations at the bottom of each article.

Seaside Park, New Jersey event: September 17, 2016, 9:30 a.m.; Manhattan Chelsea District event: September 17, 2016, 8:31 p.m.; https://en.wikipedia.org/wiki/2016_New_York_and_New_Jersey_bombings

St. Cloud, Minnesota event: September 17, 2016, 8:15 p.m.; https://en.wikipedia.org/wiki/2016_Minnesota_mall_stabbing

Burlngton, Washington event: September 23, 2016, 6:58 p.m.; https://en.wikipedia.org/wiki/2016_Cascade_Mall_shooting

Orlando, Florida event: June 12, 2016, 1:58 a.m.; https://en.wikipedia.org/wiki/2016_Orlando_nightclub_shooting

Alleged assailants (used timed or noonmark, natal, progressed, diurnal):

Ahmad Rahimi: January 23, 1988, Kabul Afghanistan, noonmark; https://en.wikipedia.org/wiki/2016_New_York_and_New_Jersey_bombings

Dahir A. Adin: accurate info unknown, born circa 1994, shot at Minnesota mall; https://en.wikipedia.org/wiki/2016_Minnesota_mall_stabbing

Arcan Certin: August 20, 1996, noonmark; https://en.wikipedia.org/wiki/2016_Cascade_Mall_shooting

Omar Mateen: November 16, 1986, 7:00 p.m., Queens, New York; https://en.wikipedia.org/wiki/2016_Orlando_nightclub_shooting; http://www.nytimes.com/interactive/2016/06/19/us/mateen-b-c.html?_r=1

Government Sources: I previously researched U.S. statehood and original capitals using encyclopedia and government websites to develop a reliable spreadsheet of info. State capitals changed frequently in our developing country. A current copy of my statehood research has been sent to AFA. It will always be a work in progress.

Originating list: http://www.50states.com

I researched individual city incorporation dates via state and municipal websites. In some instances the municipalities were incorporated prior to statehood. Location municipality. Noonmark charts are traditional for business, municipality purposes.

I researched several speculative birth times for the Declaration of Independence and based my book: Presidents of Hope and Change on the Virgo rising chart.

U.S. Virgo rising: natal, progressed, and diurnal were used; July 4, 1776, 9:36 a.m., Philadelphia, Pennsylvania

Seaside Park incorporation: natal, progressed, and diurnal were used; noonmark, May 3, 1898, Seaside Park, New Jersey

New Jersey statehood: natal, progressed, and diurnal were used; noonmark, December 18, 1787, Trenton, New Jersey

Manhattan incorporation: natal, progressed, and diurnal were used; noonmark, February 2, 1653

New York Statehood: natal, progressed, and diurnal were used; noonmark, July 26, 1788, New York City

St. Cloud incorporation: natal, progressed, and diurnal were used; noonmark, April 2, 1856, St. Cloud, Minnesota

Minnesota statehood: natal, progressed, and diurnal were used; noonmark, May 11, 1858, St. Paul, Minnesota

Burlington, Washington incorporation: natal, progressed, and diurnal were used; noonmark, June 18, 1902, Burlington,

Washington

Washington statehood: natal, progressed, and diurnal were used; noonmark, November 11, 1889, Olympia, Washington

Orlando, Florida incorporation: natal, progressed, and diurnal were used; noonmark, July 31, 1875, Orlando, Florida

Florida statehood: natal, progressed, and diurnal were used; noonmark, March 3, 1845, Tallahassee, Florida

Pulse Nightclub incorporation: natal, progressed, and diurnal were used; May 19, 2003, 8:00 a.m. (time stamped), Tallahassee, Florida; source: Electronic Articles of Organization for Florida Limited Liability Co

Mention of singer Christina Grimmie shooting 27 hours prior to Orlando, Florida massacre: June 10, 2016, 10:45 p.m., Orlando, Florida; Christina Grimmie: March 12, 1994, 10:14 a.m., Marlton, New Jersey; Shooter: Kevin James Loibi, no birth information found, suicide at event;

https://en.wikipedia.org/wiki/Christina_Grimmie

https://en.wikipedia.org/wiki/Terrorism_in_the_United_States#2010.E2.80.93present

About the Authors

José Luis Belmonte

José Luis Belmonte is an international lecturer and author of four books and research articles for the AFA Journal of Research. He is currently working on his dissertation for a master's degree in anthropology (cultural astrology and astronomy) at Wales University. He studied for an M.A. in astrology at Kepler College from 2007 until 2011, and also studied telecommunications engineering, specializing in electronic equipment, at Ramon Llull University. José also teaches astrology and researches the history of Babylonian and Hellenistic astrology, business astrology, and archetypes. He lives in Barcelona, Spain with his wife and daughter.

Alphee Lavoie

For almost half a century Alphee Lavoie, NCGR IV has earned his living as a successful full-time counseling and teaching astrologer. He held the position of NCGR research director for 12 years and pioneered many inroads in research. He has lectured all over the world at major conferences and has been nominated five times for the research and innovations award presented at UAC. Alphee is the author of three books on horary and writes a monthly horary column for Dell Horoscope. His company, AIR Software, offers 16 pieces of innovative, one-of-a-kind astrological software and the award-winning Astro financial software. Alphee is world renown as a leader in financial astrology, appearing in Bloomberg magazine and CNN broadcasts for the merits of his financial programs and expertise for accurate financial predictions. Alphee conducts astro financial seminars and teaches weekly mentoring classes at his live online astrology school, sharing his 52 years as a full time professional astrologer. He is currently conducting important, extensive astrological research with his Astro Investigators group. This group, better known as The

Gators, was founded by Alphee 14 years ago and today has 30 members, many of whom are international (www.astroinvestigators.com). Contact Alphee at www.alphee.com, alphee@comcast.net, 860-232-6521, or 800-659-1247.

Jagdish Maheshri

Jagdish Maheshri has served as NCGR research director since 2010. A contemporary Vedic astrologer, he has published and presented papers at the Baltimore and Philadelphia NCGR conferences. and was a UAC speaker in 2012. He recently spoke at a conference in New Delhi and won the outstanding global astrologer award. His current research interests are in natural and man-made calamities. Jagdish holds a Ph.D., teaches (online) Vedic astrology, is the author of several articles, appears on radio shows, and hosts his Web site, www.astroinsight.com. In 1995, he discovered a unique Ninefold Progression technique that is explained in his book It's All in Timing. He can be reached at jmaheshri@astroinsight.com.

Branimira Maldeghem

Branimira Maldeghem has an M.A. in political science and public administration, and has worked as a consultant for various NGOs and political parties in Bulgaria. For the past 12 years she has served as a policy advisor on economic and monetary affairs to a member of the European Parliament. Having been involved in both drafting and negotiating legislative proposals in the field of financial services, taxation, competition policy and consumer protection, she has developed comprehensive expertise in the institutional architecture and decision-making processes of the European Union. Branimira is passionate about psychological astrology and she is currently enrolled in a diploma programme at the Academy of AstroPsychology and Mercury Internet School of Psychological Astrology (MISPA). She is particularly fascinated by the theoretical model of AstroPsychology as developed by Glenn

Perry, Ph.D., and in exploring the psychological dynamics underlying the charts of various artists through the lenses of AstroPsychology and the manner these are reflected in real life experiences and artistic works.

Marilyn J. Muir

Marilyn Muir, LPMAFA, has been a professional astrologer and instructor for more than 40 years, and has had her own radio and television shows and a variety of astrological columns. She has been a speaker at several national conferences and astrological groups and a writer for both online and print periodicals and research journals, She is a past president of the South Florida Astrological Association and founder of Mission: Aquarius, Inc., a metaphysical church and school founded in 1978. Her books in print or e-book are *Astrology: The Symbolic Language* and *Presidents of Hope and Change*. Several more books are scheduled for publication in 2017, including *The Astrology of Coma, Tarot: The Symbolic Language*, *Numberology: The Symbolic Language*, *Astrological Choices* and *The Family* (astrological relationships). Marilyn lives in central Florida and can be reached at inspiremebks@gmail.com.

Safron Rossi

Safron Rossi, Ph.D., is an associate core faculty member at Pacifica Graduate Institute in the Jungian and archetypal studies M.A./Ph.D. program, teaching courses on mythology, archetypal symbolism, and research. For many years she was the curator at Opus Archives, which holds the Joseph Campbell and James Hillman manuscript collections. Safron is editor of *Joseph Campbell's Goddesses: Mysteries of the Feminine Divine* (New World Library, 2013) and co-editor of the forthcoming *Jung on Astrology* (Routledge, 2017). Her Web site is www.thearchetypaleye.com.

Sylvia Sky

Sylvia Sky began studying astrology in 1976. Her articles have been published in *American Astrology* and *Today's Astrologer*, and she wrote a monthly horoscope column for *St. Louis Magazine*. A professional freelance writer, she provides online sites with educational and service articles about astrology and tarot. She is the author of *Sun Sign Confidential: The Dark Side of All 12 Zodiac Signs,* and *Bonded and Hitting It Off*, a study of the characters and synastry in *Fifty Shades of Grey*. Both books are available at Amazon.com. Sylvia has a B.A. in journalism and an M.A. in English Literature.

Kyösti Tarvainen

Kyösti Tarvainen is a retired mathematics researcher and teacher. He earned a M.Sc. in technical mathematics from Helsinki Technical University and a Ph.D. in systems engineering from Case Western Reserve University. He is an emeritus docent in systems analysis at the Systems Analysis Laboratory, Helsinki Technical University. While studying in the U.S., he listened to radio programs hosted by John Manolesco, who sometimes answered questions based on the astrological chart of the listener. This aroused an interest in studying astrology. Kyösti joined the Finnish Astrological Society, and later served as its president for seven years. Due to his mathematical expertise it was natural that statistical studies became his special area in astrology.

Aureal Williams

Aureal Williams' extensive work with natural cycles has led her to the direct experience of Body as Timer. As a consultant, speaker, teacher and writer, she helps clients align with natural cycles for optimal personal energy management. Through a kinesthetic body experience, she "recovered" the Personal Lunar Cycle, a pattern of energy based on the phase of the

Moon in which one is born. In addition to teachings and consultations on the Personal and Collective Lunar Cycles, she offers the Void of Course Moon Club, a membership educational and support service for planning and scheduling around Void Moon times for optimal self-care and resource management. She writes a weekly blog post on Natural Time and Intuition, www.aurealwilliams.com/blog and can be reached at aureal@aurealwilliams.com and 513-706-7332.

Karni Zor

Karni Zor has been practicing and teaching astrology since 2000. She started her work in Israel and now speaks, lectures, and conducts astrology workshops and courses globally. Karni founded the Holistic Astrology Center and School, and is the creator of Holistic Astrological Cards being used worldwide for reading and healing sessions. The cards have been translated into seven languages (Spanish, English, Hebrew, Chinese, Dutch, French, Portuguese). Karni has a B.A. in archaeology and an M.A. in theological studies. She is married and the mother of two children.